Interning 101

Interning 101

Emily White

Interning 101
Written by: Emily White

FIRST EDITION
For permission requests, write to the publisher, addressed "Attention: Permissions Coordinator," via the Website below.

 9GiantStepsBooks
Beverly Farms, MA
www.9giantstepsbooks.com

Ordering Information:
Special discounts are available on quantity purchases by corporations, associations, and others. For details, contact the publisher via the website above.
For U.S. trade bookstores and wholesalers order, please contact the publisher via the website above.

Printed in the United States of America

Library of Congress Cataloging-in-Publication data
White, Emily.
Interning 101 / Emily White.
ISBN: 0692861181
ISBN 13: 9780692861189

To my family.
And all interns: past, present & future.

Acknowledgments

Much love, deep gratitude, and special thanks to:

Ann & Bob White, Jesse White, Grandma & Grampa White, Tish Kehoe, Grandpa Kehoe (RIP), Winifred Chane, Jill Coy, Joyce Dollinger, Amanda Palmer, Brian Viglione, Mike Luba, ChaChi Loprete, Oedipus, Ed Valauskas, Matthew Friedberger, Keri Smith Esguia, Katrina Bleckley, David Avery, Chewy Smith, Laura Keating, Melissa Garcia, Jim Anderson, Leon Janikian, Roy Coates, George Howard, Jennifer Howe, 9GiantStepsBooks, Mark Kates, Elizabeth Freund, Imogen Heap, Justin Kalifowitz, Eric Sherman, Jennica Bisbee, Bob Ezrin, Kate Turk, David Macias, Matt Holt, Dottie DeHart, DeHart & Company, Anthony Mattero, Anthony Ervin, Elwood & Dustin Tynes, Lauren Davis, Cecelia Dempsey, Coach Molly Geraldson, Bob Jenkyns, Noel Gallagher, Paul King, Briana Dougherty Chester, Elif Mills, Emma Willis, Kevin Avery, Paul Adams, Steve Ferguson, Katie Ruark, Josh Frankfort, Brendon Downey, BriAnna Olson, Michael Pope, Kay Hanley, David Bason, Greg Dempsey, Theodore Dempsey, Heather Greidanus, Melanie Nold, Kelsey McLaughlin, Beth Kahn, Jasmine LaRue, Daniel(son) Schiffer, Lorene Pillin, Megan Vick, Mikayla Foote, Carl Carpenter, Lucy Briggs, Jessica Weigand, Molly Moltzen, Michael James, Mandy Cuesta, and all of the interns I've ever had the pleasure of working with!

Table of Contents

About the Author

Emily White launched her first company, Whitesmith Entertainment, with business partner Keri Smith in 2009. Based in New York and Los Angeles, Whitesmith has overseen the careers of countless musicians and comedians to global acclaim resulting in Grammy nominated albums and Emmy Award winning writing. Whitesmith expanded into sports in 2012. Working with some of the best athletes in the world, White co-founded tech start-up Dreamfuel, supporting athletes and receiving unsolicited press in *Fast Company, Forbes, Bloomberg*, and more for the company's innovative work. As a deeply respected thought leader in both music and sports, White proudly sits on the boards of Future of Music, CASH Music, The David Lynch Foundation Live and SXSW, while additionally serving on The Recording Academy New York Chapter's Education Committee and Pandora's Artist Advisory Council. *Interning 101* is Emily White's debut book.

Foreword

CHOOSE FOR MILIEU (mil'yōō, mil'yə(r)/; *plural* milieus *or* mi-
lieux; the physical or social setting in which something occurs or
develops: environment)

By Amanda Palmer of The Dresden Dolls

I got my very first internship at age 17, when I was a senior in high school.
It's a lost chapter that I can barely recall, and it's something I forgot
about completely until I sat down to ponder the Ways of Interning. Which
is weird. I've written scores of articles and a book and done thousands
of interviews, and it only now occurs to me that I've never mentioned it
ONCE.

Why not? Because I learned absolutely nothing. I got nothing out of
it. My fault? Their fault? It's worth pondering.

Lexington High School, my suburban alma mater in bucolic
Massachusetts, was a pretty progressive high school as far as these
things go, and all seniors were encouraged, for one semester, to take
one day a week off classes (Friday, if memory serves) and take "an internship." Any internship. If you didn't take the internship, you had to go to
class. SWEET. And I remember thinking this was a golden ticket through
some kind of door into my future as a musician, so I followed my instincts
and phoned KOOLIO Records (name withheld for kindness' sake), a local

indie record label I'd vaguely heard of, and asked if they were looking for interns. "Sure," they said. "Come on in."

So in I came, ready to join the world of adults, cool record biz people, and the moving-shaking magical musical indie world of KOOLIO Records. I wasn't certain what I was in for, but I was sure I'd be delighted by the millions of useful and intriguing things I would learn. I put on my coolest punk work outfit, donned my Doc Martens, and feistily shook the hand of Steve—or whatever his name was—who answered the door at KOOLIO. I was going to have an adventure! I was working at a record label! I would LEARN THINGS! I WOULD LIVE THE DREAM!

I was wrong. Honestly: It just sucked. I showed up on the first day and was put alone in the back stock room to peel the longboxes off of 6,000 CDs. (Longboxes were a trend in the early age of CD sales—a giant wasteful cardboard house for your CD to make the artwork more appealing and the CDs less stealable.)

I sat there in the back room, along with my X-ACTO knife, for five hours, surrounded by towers of sad overstocked CDs, and peeled pieces of plastic out of cardboard. Alone. Then I took the subway and the bus home. Next week would be better!

The following week they said they didn't have anything for me to do, and I could take the day off. So I spent the day smoking clove cigarettes in Harvard Square coffee shops and shopping for used records. That day I felt better.

The next week I showed up and Steve-or-whoever told me they didn't have anything for me to do. So I smoked more cloves.

The next week I called ahead of time and asked for Steve-or-whoever, and Steve-or-whoever told me not to bother to come in. That day, I think, I decided to do psychedelic drugs and go for a walk around the Lexington conservation land.

For the next three Fridays of the semester, I called KOOLIO dutifully. They never had any work. Eventually I stopped calling. It was awesome, though, I argued to myself. I got to skip school and nobody cared! I lied to my parents, did more psychedelic drugs at the town pond, hung out with truant skateboarders, and generally wasted my life.

I look back and wish I'd realized that the whole exercise wasn't about what I could get away with, but where I could have gotten to. I wish I'd called KOOLIO, quit (quit? well, you know...), and gotten myself a new internship at the MIT Media Lab, or the Boston Anarchist Bookstore, or the Puppetry Library (all places I wasn't aware of at the time, but we're in fantasy mode here).

Unless you strike gold, no internship is going to be the thrilling, wonderful, life-changing experience you might be hoping for. You may find yourself in a basement, opening boring boxes. But if time goes by and the internship isn't feeding your brain or heart or psyche in some manner, consider what you're actually getting out of the experience. And if you gotta...leave. I hesitate to say this in the current climate of over-privileged kids demanding that their internships entertain, delight (and pay?) them... but I've also been there myself, and so: You have my personal permission to quit your internship if it truly sucks.

But, truth: It isn't supposed to be all thrills and unicorns. Don't underestimate the small silver linings of a shitty job, and with that, I'll tell you the story of my next internship, which also sucked a little, but way less than KOOLIO. This internship came about while I was abroad in Germany during college. I was way into experimental theater at the time. Much like my high school internship, I got an internship at a weird little theater by cold-asking. I convinced someone local to Cologne to post me a newspaper a few months before I arrived, I looked at the theater listings, found the weirdest theater, and called them, asking if I could intern there. "Sure!" they said. "Come on over."

My internship at the KOOLHAUS THEATRE was several days a week, and this time I was given much more interesting tasks. I was making coffee for the staff and director, hanging out in the patio of the theater, watching the flow of the workday. I was opening up the theater before rehearsals (although that task was revoked and the key taken back promptly after I snuck into the theater one night to try to play their piano and accidentally woke one of the actors—fat, chain-smoking Helmut, who was sleeping on a couch upstairs from the main stage because he was then homeless). I often sat in the office and stamped stacks of envelopes, but I got to listen in on the office gossip (which, by the by, improved my German greatly). One day I got to apply sequin sparkles to drag platform shoes because the house costumier needed an extra pair of hands.

The work itself was scut-work, and mind-numbingly boring, but that didn't actually matter. The memories and impressions I have of those three months of my life aren't about the coffee or the envelopes; they're about the other things I saw and smelled. The way these people all worked together. The stress of running a small theater and their desperation for funding. The hot tattooed girl at the box office who invited me out for beers one day and became my first lesbian one-night-stand. The ability to see *Hamletmachine* by Heiner Müller multiple times without having to pay. The stories that the costumier told me about her children while we sat and applied sequins. The vision of fat, chain-smoking Helmut shouting at me from the top of the stairs in his filthy bathrobe that fateful piano night. These beautiful images are seared into my memory and are the sequined moments of a life well-lived.

If there's a moral here, I suppose it's this: If you're going to be an intern, choose for milieu. Choose for environment over prestige. Choose for scene over box content. You're going to be doing relatively annoying unpaid work; that's the reality of the intern. So check out the vibe, the human people, the room in which you'll sit, and make sure it's going to provide you with some meaningful stories. You'll never remember the coffee or the boxes, but you'll remember Helmut, not Steve-or-whoever.

Amanda Palmer
Woodstock, NY
September 2016

Introduction

When I went to college, I could not wait to intern. I chose to attend Northeastern University in Boston, known for their experiential learning and academics, so I could alternate semesters between classroom study and gaining real-world experience in my desired field.

Growing up in the 1990s, I dreamed of a career in the music industry. At the time, it seemed logical that the first step would be interning at a record company. It was hard to believe that I would gain college credit to fulfill my dreams, as interning was encouraged as part of Northeastern's acclaimed cooperative education program.

The advice from my university professors and advisors was simple: **As an intern, make yourself indispensable while simultaneously observing and immersing yourself in the field.** This single piece of advice is the most essential to interns. While I hope this creed is still taught in schools, as a business owner who has observed many student interns over the past decade, it is clear that students are not being given the required knowledge to transition seamlessly from school to the workplace.

As someone who is half Millennial and half Generation X (I was born in 1982, on the border of these two generations), I grew up on Winona Ryder films and Nirvana, yet I am extremely fluent with technology. In true Millennial style, I became CEO of my own company at age 25. That said, there was no way I could have launched my own business in my mid-20s without the experiences I gained from my internships.

After graduating from Northeastern University employed in the music industry, I could not wait to work with interns. I thought it would be fun to work with eager students who were ready to learn our field. I would be the young professional in the office who always made sure they could get into our concerts and events, as I was grateful for such things during my interning days.

Throughout the years I have mentored some very impressive interns. I make it clear in interviews that interning for me and my company is challenging. For instance, we expect interns to do everything we ask of them within 24 business hours. If they cannot achieve this for any reason, that is totally fine. They need to tell their supervisor so everyone is on the same page.

I bring this up at every interview with prospective interns and they all chuckle. Many respond, "Of course; that's what interning is." Despite this, roughly half of the interns who come through our program fail to do this. Even though this requirement is clearly stated in our interviews and is later reinforced, a disconnect exists and must be dealt with. Like many companies, clear communication among team members at all levels is the foundation of our business.

More recently, a struggling intern had a revelation midway through the semester: "I realize that I have never done anything for myself until now. Everything has been done for me my entire life." This realization came from a graduate student attending a prestigious university; this was the student's first step toward career reality. She is now thriving both personally and professionally on account of the critical thinking and problem solving skills she developed from interning.

The students who intern for us flourish, with many going on to successful jobs in their desired fields. Some even start their own companies. The interns who succeed are those who understand and master the tenets in this book; these principles are applicable in a variety of fields.

Here is a breakdown of what an internship is. During an internship, you receive training in a particular field; you attain real-life experience that prepares you for higher-level work once you complete your internship. This process is never-ending, because you continually build your professional network and are always learning and growing at all stages of life. As a student intern, you train for your craft, obtaining crucial skills to prepare you for your career and beyond. Furthermore, interning can launch you into your field. The following is what an internship is not.

Over the past few years, I have seen the concept of internships evolve from an opportunity for professional enhancement and growth to the expectation that interning is a direct pipeline to a job. This misconception generally manifests in two thoughts on the part of the intern: *1. If I intern at a company long enough, I'll get hired. 2. If an employer sees an internship on my résumé, I'll get hired.*

Scenario one can and does happen. More often, an internship is a gateway into a field, not a specific company. Most companies could never realistically take on all of the interns who come through their door each year. If there happens to be an opening when you happen to be graduating and looking for a job, you are certainly in a better position to fill that opening in comparison to an external applicant. But those are slim odds, and the goal of this book is to broaden your chances for success.

What employers *can* do is introduce interns to other companies through events and the tasks they do during their internship. I remember one highly respected colleague talking about my now co-manager, Melissa, when she was an intern. He recommended I hire her because he could see as an intern how strong she was in multiple areas. The fact that this colleague even knew of Melissa's work is a testament to Melissa's putting herself out there in a professional, hardworking, helpful, and effective manner. Clearly if I had not hired Melissa, one of my other colleagues would have, based on the skills she demonstrated as an intern.

Hiring from within certainly does happen, but this will occur only if the intern has an understanding of the company's culture. Deepening your knowledge of a company's core goals and ideals, both small and large, is arguably as important as any business skill. To increase your odds of "being in the right place at the right time" when a job arises, ensure you have proven yourself to be the right person.

This requires that you work both hard and effectively. Do everything that is asked of you to the best of your ability while constantly learning and thinking about what you are doing and how it plugs into the bigger picture. If you cannot ascertain how a task that seems menial connects to the bigger picture, choose a quiet moment late in the workday or at a social work function and ask a relevant staff member for clarification.

Your supervisor may not have time to break it down while the task is happening, but know that everything done at a company, even something as simple as a database entry, affects someone else around you. So do it well and do it right. Take pride in all the tasks you are given, even getting lunch for someone. I will discuss how to thrive by completing what may seem like menial tasks in Chapter 7, and explain how they are not as obsequious as an intern might initially think.

While internships will help you break into your field in the "real world," you have to make genuine connections and contacts during your internship that will help grow your career step by step. Having internships on a résumé can and will get you in the door for an interview. All the same, you will need real and applicable up-to-date professional skills obtained through internships to help land and keep a job.

If your internship resulted only in a company's name on a piece of paper, your prospects of landing a job are, unfortunately, as thin as a piece of paper. I have never used a traditional résumé in my professional career. My first internship was obtained through my university's database. That led to more experiences and internships that blossomed into my actual career. This may not be your specific path, but the point is, take advantage of the resources around you to get started (which we will delve into throughout this book), and build on top of that once you are out there.

The good news is interning is a proven path to success for countless executives and people at all levels of the workforce. Some of my favorite intern success stories include Gary Dell'Abate, better known as "Baba Booey" of *The Howard Stern Show*. As executive producer of the show since 1984, Dell'Abate earned his start by getting lunch for Howard (I will talk about the benefits of running an errand like this in Chapter 7). Multi-Oscar winner Tom Hanks entered his field by interning at The Great Lakes Theater Festival in Cleveland. Filmmaker Spike Lee was an intern for Columbia Pictures. Oprah Winfrey, arguably one of the most successful people in history, began working in television as an intern for a Nashville CBS affiliate.

Internships exist to teach the methods of a field, to begin building a professional network (both online and off), and to gain real-life experience. There is an exchange that requires professionals to take time out of their incredibly busy days to teach interns crucial skills that they can then apply to their own careers. Learning a trade from a working professional is exactly what interning is all about. I will discuss how this learning can be both direct and indirect, as there is much to be gained even if your supervisor is not (or does not have the time to be) mentoring you in a way that you envisioned.

In highly competitive fields, such as entertainment, where *many* people want to get their foot in the door, interns who are paid come in with skills to justify their compensation. I have never had an intern show up with these skills; which is exactly the point of the internship. Over the past decade, this apprenticeship trade has come under fire. I will discuss the pros, cons, and benefits (yes, the benefits!) of an unpaid internship, and how to survive and thrive irrespective of whether or not you receive financial support from your internship.

As an intern, a friend of mine who now runs an extremely successful music publishing company used to read the major label contracts that he was tasked with making copies of. By doing this, he learned the ins and outs of how a legal agreement for a major pop star works. Interns need to observe the office environment and the conversations their bosses are having with people. They need to observe *who* they are talking to and be mindful of the people who come in and out of the office. Working virtually? Read all messages from the bottom up to not miss a single nugget of information.

If the supervisors of the company you are interning for have nothing for you to do, it may be because they have so much going on that they do not even have time to delegate. This is a great position to be in. Take it all in, observe, and read Chapter 7 to figure out ways you can contribute that benefit both you and the company.

Similarly, though, I believe completing internships is important because you never know what will come of them. If you leave and do not have a great experience, maybe working at that company or in that particular part of the field is not for you. Maybe the field is not what you thought it would be, and pursuing something else or something in another area within your field makes sense. It is equally as important in internships to learn what you do not want to do as it is to obtain skills and work toward a career that is right for you.

This is a preview of some of the advice I will give throughout the book to help you succeed in your internships and beyond. This book will offer tips in a handy format, giving you a leg up before you begin an internship as well as a prodigious start to your career path.

A note on **HOW TO USE THIS BOOK**: I've tried to give guidance throughout *Interning 101* to help you jump around if you'd like to focus on specific areas of your interning process, so you'll see a bit of "For more on X, head over to Chapter X." That said, it's really not that long of a book, and the best interns achieve success by understanding each step of the process, not skipping steps along the way. If that mentality is one you don't generally consider, try it with this book and see what happens.

At the same time, I'm not egotistical enough to assume that you might want to know how I navigated my way through and to the top of the music industry. There are a slew of practical tips throughout the first four chapters exemplified through my personal experiences. But if you are already at your internship and are feeling a little lost on how to do certain tasks, Chapters 5 and after are the nitty-gritty basics of how to perform various tasks that may be asked of you at your internship. I have tried to make this book an easily digestible guide for you—while keeping it as short as possible. With that in mind, you can also use the past two paragraphs as a quick guide if you happen to be extra pressed for time and/or want to hone in on any specific areas you know you need to focus in on.

One

My Story

Don't Be Above Anything. Instead Go Above & Beyond by Saying Yes to Everything.

I grew up in the village of Hartland, Wisconsin. One wonderful thing about being a Millennial born to Baby Boomers is that our parents told us we could be whatever we wanted to be when we grew up. We could be astronauts, teachers, professional athletes, or the president of the United States. No matter our gender or race, any of these vocations were now attainable with the right education and a strong work ethic.

Despite my parents' approval, when I made the conscious decision to set out and work in the music industry, I will never forget a classmate in high school sarcastically announcing to the class: "Yeah...good luck with that."

My classmate had a point: It *was* going to be a long and hard journey to break into a field that was nonexistent to anyone living in a southeastern Wisconsin suburb, but I figured we all have to start somewhere.

Growing up as Millennials, our parents, teachers, and other role models always encouraged us to find something we love and pursue it. In my life that something was music. In middle school I was voted most likely to become a roadie. (A decade later I was a tour manager for bands, which in many ways is a roadie.) When I was not swimming competitively, I spent much of my time earning money to buy albums and attend concerts. I dreamed of moving to England and camping outside of the office of Marcus Russell, who manages the band Oasis, until he would let me help in any way possible. (Years later, the fact that Marcus has always been nothing but kind to me still makes me smile.)

When I began exploring college programs in 1997, all I could find were music or music therapy degrees. I was not a talented musician despite years of lessons and many futile attempts to write songs, so none of these academic fields seemed like the right fit. It was the early days of the Internet, and I was on a listserv (essentially a message board) for hardcore Oasis fans. A regular contributor to the list apologized one day for being away (she was generally great at finding obscure news and content), as she had been diligently applying to colleges. She was thrilled to announce she had been accepted to Northeastern University's Music Industry program. I immediately knew that was going to be my major. I had never heard of the school or this particular major, so I began researching at that very moment.

It turned out that Northeastern was located in Boston, which was a major market for concerts. (Much to my dismay, international bands in particular often skipped nearby Milwaukee, which is the closest city to where I grew up.) In addition, the university had a Division I women's swimming team. A swimming scholarship was my best hope to pay for an out-of-state, private college.

I continued to research the school and found Northeastern touting its "co-op program" as a way to develop tangible professional skills no matter the field. Co-op is short for cooperative education and is basically the same as interning. Students are encouraged and oftentimes required to alternate semesters working in their desired fields with semesters of academic work. Through experiential learning, students begin building real-life skills, knowledge, and professional networks prior to graduating. I could not believe there was a school that would offer me college credit to intern at a record company, which would be a dream come true at the time.

BREAKING THROUGH BARRIERS AND BREAKING SCHOOL RECORDS: AN UNSTOPPABLE WORK ETHIC EARNS ME A DREAM DEGREE

It was not going to be easy to attend a $30,000+/year school 1,000 miles away from home. I knew I wanted to swim competitively in college because I had been on teams since I was three, I had trained seriously since middle school, and I enjoyed swimming. But even with my strong athletic background, securing a swimming scholarship was not a given. My times were good but not earth-shattering. I contacted Northeastern's coach, and much to my delight he responded.

In 1998 Northeastern was a good, mid-level Division I swimming team, a contender in their conference. Yet if I chose this school, I would not have to prioritize my swimming ahead of my academic life and career (no one ever says that officially at larger sports schools, but you get the idea). No doubt I would have to work incredibly hard to achieve times worthy of a swimming scholarship at Northeastern, but the goal was attainable because the program was strong, yet they weren't necessarily recruiting Olympians.

So I worked hard. Extremely hard. Each day at swim practice, I thought about how much I wanted to work in the music industry. Lo and behold, my times began to drop, and I was offered a 75 percent scholarship to attend Northeastern University, the school of my dreams. I ended up working so hard that by the time I walked on to campus and competed in my first meet, I broke a school record, prompting the coach to immediately move me up to a full scholarship. I mention these results because they came out of sheer hard work, a work ethic that would later define my career.

By sophomore year I was excited and ready for my first internship. The university had a handful of local listings for music industry companies in the Boston area. I applied at a few and quickly narrowed the field down to Powderfinger Promotions, a college radio-oriented company that also handled public relations and marketing campaigns for bands. Note that I did another interview at a company that shall

3

remain unnamed, who forgot they were even interviewing an intern that day. That's ok! I barely remember that moment looking back. But again, it's good to get out of your comfort zone in early days and have both positive and not so great moments interviewing. Get these experiences under your belt while you're in school; instead of after graduation.

A great thing about interning is that you get some jitters out of your system because you are thrown into various new work experiences. The end result of such exposure is that you feel more confident when you are in similar situations after graduating from college, as mentioned. For example, despite being a confident and outgoing person, I was very nervous for my interview at Powderfinger.

The office was really cool, adorned with images of various albums, bands, and tour posters. I was interviewed by an equally cool young woman named Winifred Chane. I was able to relax a little when I discovered that she too was from the Midwest. (This is a great question to ask in interviews and in general when networking: where someone is from. People love to talk about themselves, and you might find some common ground to get the conversation going; the latter of which is what happened in my interview with Winifred.)

MY LONG-ANTICIPATED INTERNSHIP BEGINS

I left my interview at Powderfinger with a stack of CDs (which was the best thing ever in that era), and I returned to the dorms to wait to hear from them. This was right at the cusp of email becoming commonplace and I now encourage you to send a concise thank-you email the business day after your interview (maybe wait till Monday if that business day happens to be a Friday).

I ended up getting the internship and I could not wait to report to work each day to help out Winifred and her boss, David Avery. Winifred made it clear to me that David was very nice, but he was not to be bothered. He was a very busy and well-connected person who had been working in the industry for a long time.

David asked me to pick up his lunch for him every day, and always would insist that he pay for my lunch. (When your boss offers to pay for your coffee, food, etc., say yes! I have too many interns turn me down on this, which is ridiculous. Just politely accept and respond with genuine gratitude.)

At the time, I could not believe David would have someone get his lunch for him. Now I understand! I certainly have days when I am drowning in work that is far more time sensitive and important than sparing even a few minutes to order lunch. I ask interns to order for me only if I truly do not have the time so I can stay focused on the work at hand, and (of course) I buy them whatever they want as well.

If your boss asks you to pick up lunch or coffee, know that you are helping the company because that is time your supervisor can use to focus on moving work forward. Listen in on whatever it is your supervisors are working on that causes them to not have time to order or sometimes even to eat. That is what you are there for, which is an opportunity many interns miss. **Listen, watch, and observe what the professionals are doing and how they do it. You will gain insight into the field and pick up business etiquette skills as well as company / industry culture cues along the way.**

Interning at Powderfinger involved more than buying the company founder's lunch. In order to promote the bands, we regularly mailed out their CDs to college radio stations. Winifred would give me a list of stations to call each day asking if they had received the CD package we had sent them. If they had, I asked them for feedback on a list of songs and encouraged the program director to play them.

I was terrified. *Calling people?* More specifically, cool music industry people whom I dreamed of working with?? Scary. Regardless, I dug in and managed to get through my call list day after day, eventually prompting Winifred to say that I was one of the best interns they'd ever had. This baffled me, as *all I did was what she asked of me.*

Sadly and amazingly, doing what you are supposed to do while being accountable for yourself will take you at least halfway along the road to success in most situations. But you need to go even further; do not do only the things you are supposed to do. Do those things that you say you'll do, and you will begin building a reputation for being reliable. I would hire someone for that trait alone—reliability—because it is so important to our company and to the field in general.

As I got to know Winifred better, I mentioned to her once after work that I was nervous calling the radio stations. She kindly laughed and said that the program directors I was calling were also college students, so in fact they were my peers. After this conversation, I was more at ease calling the radio stations during my internship at Powderfinger. More significantly, though, by the end of my internship, I never feared using the phone in a professional situation again. As an executive today, I have scheduled calls every hour on the hour some days. Phone skills are now at the core of conducting my business on a daily basis and something I do with ease.

In addition to doing everything that was asked of me at Powderfinger, a key to my success was also saying yes to every concert to which I was invited. This may sound like a no-brainer because I enjoyed going to live shows. In reality, this meant I said yes to concerts that were genres I was not necessarily into and would not go to as a fan or for leisure.

The result? Winifred and I ended up being show buddies and still are to this day. At the gigs, Winifred would introduce me to everyone she knew. I continued to not only develop professional relationships with industry people I met at shows, but by the time I graduated from Northeastern, I knew pretty much everyone in the Boston music scene. Additionally, my comfort level within the concert scene and work-related scenarios at events continued to grow.

As the spring semester came to a close, Winifred and Dave asked me to stick around for the summer. Even though I admired them a great deal, I had promised myself that I would never intern at the same place twice. I had already gained experience and developed professional relationships with the people at Powderfinger, but I always wanted to continue to expand professionally and gain new experiences. This meant leaving a great situation, taking a risk, and interning somewhere new.

MORE INTERNSHIPS HELP DEVELOP INSTINCTS, INDUSTRY CONTACTS, AND RESILIENCY

Next up, I applied at an indie label and recording studio on the outskirts of Boston. I was nervous to leave the comforts of Winifred and Dave at Powderfinger, but they encouraged me to spread my wings. As I mentioned, I am still in touch with both Win and Dave. Winifred is one of my best friends and is currently my neighbor in NYC, and it all goes back to our working together in Boston over a decade ago.

My interview at the label went well, and the intern supervisor offered me the internship. She seemed excited about me at the interview, and I could not wait to get started. When I reported for work the next week, there was nothing for me to do, which was in sharp contrast to my experience at Powderfinger. I offered to help the label manager with whatever she needed (we will discuss throughout the book how to find ways to help without constantly asking or getting in the way), but for some reason, in her eyes I could do no right. My supervisor appeared to be annoyed with me; though, I did not take it personally as it seemed she was not very happy in life.

> That is a good reminder across the board: **In most cases, don't take things personally in business.** It is business. If someone is stressed or short with you, generally the reason has nothing to do with you! The sooner you develop a thick skin, the better off you will be in any professional setting.

Still, I tried to make myself useful whenever I could. I tried to help the studio manager, but he was incredibly shy and quiet and that did not really get me anywhere at the time. Despite that, he turned out to be a long-term colleague I am still in touch with. Remember that even if the experience does not pan out at the time, it never hurts to at least try and help everyone you come across at an internship.

Meanwhile, I had also landed an internship across town at the legendary alternative radio station WBCN (sadly now RIP). I split my time interning a few days a week at the label and the other days at the radio station. In hindsight, that is now a strategy I strongly encourage. **By interning at two places for the semester, I was not only doubling my experience and contacts from a practical standpoint, but I could also compare and contrast the experiences as I figured out what I wanted to do within the field.** Because the music scene—as well as other industries—is relatively self-contained, many of these companies also work with each other and have staff who know and see one another regularly at shows and networking events.

At the time, WBCN was *the* station in town both nationally and locally. My interview went well with Melissa, the internship coordinator. Melissa was genuinely friendly despite the pressures of her job assisting and answering the slew of phone calls that came in for Oedipus, the station's legendary program director.

If I had this book at the time, I would have known to research everyone and everything about the places where I was interning. Instead I had no idea who Oedipus was or what he looked like. I have since discovered that Oedipus is credited with being the first DJ to play punk rock on American radio. He was also one of the first people to play The Police on air, prompting Sting to personally thank him when the band was inducted into the Rock & Roll Hall of Fame.

I was unaware of any of this on my first day as an intern at WBCN, and I could not for the life of me figure out how to use the copy machine. After trying everything I could think of and knowing that my supervisor needed the copies immediately, I asked someone walking by for help. Amazingly, that person turned out to be the legendary Oedipus, who many people in the office sometimes feared.

On the one hand, this experience shows that it does not hurt to ask for help if you have tried to figure out a task from multiple angles and are truly stuck, because you never know who you will meet. On the other, many in Oedipus's position would not have been pleased to have had their busy day interrupted with something so basic. It is therefore important to research the staff prior to your internship so you know who is who to not unwittingly bruise an ego on day one.

Interning at WBCN was remarkable. The staff members were instantly welcoming. One of my first tasks was to count out backstage passes for the big festival the station was hosting that upcoming weekend, an event with a ton of great artists on the bill.

I did my job but was incredibly nervous to ask a certain question—I thought about it all day as I was counting and organizing the backstage laminates for the event—but at the end of the day, I gathered my courage and queried. I very politely asked the fancy promotions director, whom I had been helping out, and who had been yelling at people all day, if there was any chance I could have one of the laminates, but I totally understood if the answer was no. He slipped me two and said, "Bring a friend, have fun, and thanks for your help today."

Within a few weeks at the radio station, I was regularly helping to set up the in-studio sessions with Coldplay, Tom Morello, and other artists I grew up admiring and still adore to this day. Let me be clear—"helping" usually meant ensuring everyone had a bottle of water. I want to reiterate that interning tasks are more often than not, far from glamorous. At the same time, I was learning a considerable amount every moment of every day I was at WBCN.

In contrast with my time at WBCN, during my other days interning at the record label, it still seemed like I couldn't do anything right. The intern supervisor clearly wanted nothing to do with me, there was rarely work to do, and it was often (literally) quiet during the day. Despite being a music company, they did not play music at the office. So at the time, I quietly sat at my desk, helped when I could, and listened to my own music.

I wondered if I should quit and spend all of my time at the radio station. What was the point of being at the label? It did not seem like they even wanted me around, and there wasn't much to do. Meanwhile, I was well liked at the radio station, and there was no shortage of exciting music work going on.

AN UNEXPECTED OPPORTUNITY OPENS NEW DOORS

One day at the label, a musician walked in who worked at the station part-time. His name was Ed, and he asked if I could help him put together some press kits. I happily obliged, and Ed was pleased enough with my work that he asked if I would be interested in selling T-shirts and CDs (a.k.a., "merch," an industry term that is short for merchandise) for his band that weekend at the Paradise Rock Club (my favorite venue in Boston).

He was opening for Kay Hanley from Letters to Cleo. I had always wondered how people scored jobs working at the merch table for bands and for venues. There was nothing I loved more than live music. Plus, I was a fan of Letters to Cleo, so of course I said yes and was psyched.

I set up at the venue that weekend, and from then on I was hooked on selling merch. The Paradise was laid out in such a way that I could watch the show while I kept an eye on the merch table. Ed paid me $50 for helping out. My first paid gig! I truly could not believe someone had paid me to help out at a concert—the type of event I would generally pay to attend. Eventually the band brought me on tour to regional shows throughout New England, which was not only a great experience, but also a lot of fun.

I ended up staying at both companies that summer, completing my internship at the label and the radio station successfully. Not long after, my love of live music prompted me to pursue tour management. When I eventually tour managed for a band, an experience which had an enormous impact on my life, I immediately contacted Ed.

As the business guy in his band, Ed was in charge of tour managing their shows and tours. He sent me a list of questions that I needed to ask the venues weeks before the shows to organize everything for the artist, which is called "advancing" a show. Ed turned out to be a great friend and mentor whose friendship I still cherish today.

The point here is that I made lifelong contacts out of an internship that I had considered quitting. The experience I gained working with Ed at shows and touring was as crucial—if not more valuable—to my career development than working at the radio station.

The skills and contacts I gained at WBCN were very important to my career. I was interning at a high level in a semi-corporate setting, and Oedipus remains a dear friend and inspiring mentor, as is Cha-chi who was the aforementioned Promotions Director. On the other hand, working for Ed selling merch for his band at venues, as well as learning tour managing ropes, ended up being hands-on practical skills that directly affected my career trajectory. I am grateful that I decided to stick out an internship that seemed fruitless at the time, but ended up being a significant boost to my career.

THE LESSON: RECOGNIZE THE VALUE OF EARLY IMMERSION IN YOUR FIELD OF INTEREST (EVEN WHEN IT FEELS POINTLESS)

As my story reveals, there are benefits to be gained from *all* internship and professional experiences—even if it seems terrible at the time and there is no short-term happy ending. What you gain from the experience may benefit you down the line. Additionally, a "bad" experience at an internship can illustrate what you do not want to pursue after graduation or traits you never wish to adopt when you are someday in a leadership position.

Even if a student knows exactly what they want to do, it is still beneficial to try different experiences within the desired field to gain a broad range of knowledge. You don't know what the future holds or how your career will unfold and evolve. It is hard to picture now, but what you want to do at 19 might be different from what you want to do when you are 40. You never know where you will use certain skills that you have obtained along the way.

Having a broad set of skills has allowed me to diversify into multiple disciplines of my own choosing. Over the past decade, I have parlayed my experiences in music into the fields of sport, technology, and education. This was never my plan or intention, but I could not have expanded into other areas that I am drawn to without every professional experience I have acquired to date.

KEY TAKEAWAYS

Know the players at your internship. Before your interview, research the names you'll be interning for. This will help your comfort level during the interview and give you a leg up on familiarizing yourself with the staff once you're on the job.

Observe everything. Internships are meant to be immersive, so pay attention to everything once you begin. You'll be able to pick up how the company runs just by listening, watching, and absorbing the office dynamics each day.

Work on your phone skills. Being able to speak to others with confidence and ease is a learned skill. Work on your communication techniques, speak clearly, and do your best to overcome feeling shy on the phone. Fearful of this? Don't fret; we'll get into it more in Chapter 5.

Don't be "above" the menial work. Instead complete your tasks thoughtfully. Even if you're handing out coffee or doing database entries, remember that you're contributing to the team and that each element fits together toward the greater goal. Think about how your role fits into that process, so you grasp and understand each step that you take, so in the future, you understand how all moving parts work together seamlessly. And listen—if you're doing menial work, it may be because the company is so busy they can't even take the time to delegate more. Pay attention to what's going on around you while you're completing these tasks; you'll be amazed at the knowledge you soak up.

Say "yes" to everything. Internships are full of opportunities—even if you don't immediately recognize them as such. The key is to say yes whenever you're invited to help out, participate, or show up at a work event. You never know when an important door could open that leads to something big, and regardless, you are gaining experience and building your network either way.

Go above and beyond. Doing what is asked of you is a commonsense way to rise to the top. But take it one step further and always do whatever you say you'll do. If you stick to your word and complete tasks on time and without your supervisor having to follow-up, you will begin building a reputation as a dependable and conscientious worker.

Let the boss buy you lunch. If your supervisor wants you to pick up her lunch and offers to pay for yours as well, let her! Be gracious, say thank you, and enjoy it!

Two

The Interning Struggle

Let's Get This Straight: I'm Not a Rich Kid. How to Survive and Thrive in an Unpaid Internship.

As I mentioned earlier, I could not wait to intern when I was in college. To me, interning in the music business was synonymous with fun. When I was growing up, it seemed like many adults loathed their jobs. When our teachers and parents told us to find something we love and make it a career, I listened to them and believed I could truly follow my bliss and make a rewarding career out of it. My path led to music.

The idea of working at a job that supported musicians and their craft while listening to music all day and attending concerts at night was a dream come true. However, to have access to these types of opportunities, you may have to intern without recompense (as I did) to get a foothold in an extremely competitive field. Although this means you may not earn a paycheck, if you play your cards right, you *will* walk away with a wealth of knowledge and connections that will help you build a successful and rewarding career.

As I previously mentioned, I will pay any student who shows up and has the skills necessary to do the work at my company. 99.9 percent of my experience has been that students need to be trained. This is the reason I wrote this book. As soon as we see interns contributing with skills, we pay them. Otherwise, the staff and I are taking time out of our never-ending and insanely busy days to teach and train students. Paying to teach is a luxury many companies cannot afford, if for no other reason than the time it takes away from work.

I have read that the Ford Foundation not only is able to pay their interns but specifically recruits students who come from need-based programs with high academic standards. That is AWESOME and I truly wish all companies in a position to do so put as much thought into their internship process as the Ford Foundation does.

This book is written, at its core, from the perspective of starting a DIY music company in the modern era. I could not be more proud of what my companies have achieved, and, in particular, my start-up looks to recruit from women's colleges and seeks out people of color to help close the massive hiring disparity in the tech industry. If you're a straight white guy, do not fret. We always choose the right candidate for each opportunity, but are mindful of those who might otherwise and unfairly be overlooked in various fields.

The goal of this book is to offer real-world tips on how to succeed if you do *not* come from a rich family (like me and so many others). I am privileged, no doubt, but certainly was not rolling in cash as a student from my family, who has dedicated their life to educating and working with students. This chapter provides guidance on creating opportunity based on proven tactics of how to navigate the modern business world as well as point you in the right direction on where to look for support and resources. Even if you are getting a stipend for your internship, you shouldn't assume it will be enough to live on. My experience with paid internships was that it did not cover living expenses in London or Boston by any means. Therefore, these tips are generally needed by students at both paid and unpaid internships.

No matter one's perspective on this topic, the fields my experiences are drawn from are fiercely competitive. Your industry could very well be equally sought-after. Regardless, there are ways to break through even if you're able to intern only one day a week. Crush it on that one day! And don't be shy about being open about your situation with your supervisor.

If you are working a paid job and interning, you are definitely not alone in that category and may even glean additional skills that your more well-off colleagues are missing out on (seriously).

Many students do not pursue internships as they feel they cannot afford to do so. Students may feel that all of the meaningful jobs are taken by people who can afford to intern without being paid, but at the end of the day, employers are looking for people with skills, passion, and grit. These skills are attained through diligence and hard work, or as Malcolm Gladwell states in Outliers, *10,000 hours. People who try and take shortcuts will be exposed, and those who immerse themselves in their field will continue to learn and grow while gaining a deeper understanding of their industry every day.*

If you are going to school, how are you paying for it? Take that same approach and apply it to your internships. Have you earned any sort of scholarship money? Similarly, there are a slew of grants for all types of people to help subsidize their cost of living while they intern. Look around, ask around, post around, do your research, and you will be amazed at what you come up with while simultaneously learning how to research and problem solve with tangible results.

MY SURVIVAL TALE: INTERNING IN NYC

I went to college in Boston and I wanted to intern in New York City, one of the most expensive cities in the world. I was able to achieve this goal after my junior year of college, despite the fact that I had little money and no place to live.

I found a local college, Mount Saint Mary, that housed interns for the summer at a fraction of rental prices in the city. Furthermore, I met other interns in the building who became a part of my network. Beyond that, I did all I could to keep my living expenses low. The location happened to be within walking distance of my internship, saving me subway costs. I generally made my lunch or took advantage of the city's famous (and filling) bagels. I also looked for deals like two pizza slices for $2.00 to keep my budget in line with that of a college student.

I interned in the Viacom/MTV building in Times Square. It was a competitive internship, and I was placed at VH1 Classic. Frankly, at the time I wished I was at MTV2 where the interns were helping out with Radiohead concerts and working with indie artists who were more in line with what I listened to. But as previously mentioned, all internships have value and lead to something else. For instance, my experience at VH1 Classic helped me land my first ever international job at MTV in London the following summer as well as fortuitously meet my first Beatle.

There were also other perks in addition to the professional relationships I established (which are still intact to this day). While at VH1 Classic, the producer who hired me was chosen to give a presentation to all MTV/VH1 interns one day at a luncheon. I will never forget how this successful producer explained that she had worked extremely hard during the day at her internship at VH1 and then spent her evenings and weekends waiting tables at a diner in the city.

I think about that story now and I am reminded of my current co-manager, Melissa, who was one of the best interns we have ever had. Melissa was accustomed to high-stress situations from working in a restaurant, and it is no surprise that she now has a successful and burgeoning career, not to mention that she is still in her twenties and overseeing a global artist's career.

It is easy to look at others, wonder how they obtained their position, and potentially feel resentment. Instead of feeling envious, I encourage students to reach out and ask what their path and steps were to that position. Maybe that person did land an internship through a connected friend or family member. But if they do not put in the work and grasp concepts related to the business and field, that door quickly shuts.

Work very hard and remember why you're interning in the first place. This will help you keep negative feelings at bay. Interning is an opportunity to enter virtually any field in the world. You will learn things in ways that cannot occur in the classroom. It is a time to apply what you have cultivated in life and at school in order to forge a direction in career development, and yet you are still allowed to make mistakes along the way. It is a trial period that you should take as seriously as school, knowing that missteps are permitted as they offer a learning opportunity. Though definitely learn from missteps so you do not repeat them again.

ADVENTURES IN MAKING ENDS MEET

When it comes to surviving as an unpaid intern, it may be cliché, but where there's a will, there's a way. The students I have encountered who need to figure out a means to earn additional income (which is pretty much everyone, by the way, because even "rich kids" have parents who want them to assay how they are going to survive without their help) oftentimes outdo those who do not have to resolve where and how they are going to live.

> *Interns who simultaneously work at part-time jobs also learn how to balance their time and energy between multiple gigs. As tough as that is at times, it really does make you stronger, and you will develop crucial time-management, work ethic and people skills across the board by doing so.*

It is not impossible to find a paid internship in the entertainment industry. In the United Kingdom, interns have graduated from college and are therefore always paid. The British outlook on the American structure is often negative, and I would like to clarify that the examples I highlight refer to the assumption that the student is in school and interning in the field they are studying, as is the standard in the United States.

I've mentioned that in our company's internship program, we will happily pay any intern who exhibits the skills required to do the work (which is also the law). Yet I very rarely have an intern show up with applicable workplace skills. Which is fine. That is exactly the point of an internship—for students to learn real-life competencies within in a professional setting. In rare cases, I see students grasping concepts and the tasks at hand within a few weeks, ideally within a few months, and almost always by the end of their internship.

> *If you are crushing it in your internship and you have made your-self indispensable, then you will have no problem getting paid in due time, either via your current situation or somewhere else as you build your skills and network within the field. For now, interning until you grasp the concepts of your industry and making yourself indispensable to a company is your path to success.*

When you are just beginning to climb your way up the ladder, there are ways to make unpaid internships affordable and achievable. Living in expensive cities, such as New York or Los Angeles, while working a job without a paycheck is no small task. It is possible, though. Here are some resources as you begin to plan for how you will (literally) survive during your internship.

FINDING HOUSING

Housing will be the most important and most expensive piece of the puzzle. Finding an affordable apartment in a city like New York is impossible for many working professionals, let alone students. Instead of trying to rent an apartment by yourself, consider alternative options that will be cheaper and more attainable.

UNIVERSITY HOUSING

Locate universities in the area in which you are looking to intern. Many have additional housing options available to students at discounted rates, especially during the summer. These can be ideal situations because they offer university security, and many come with communal kitchens so you can save money by preparing meals at home. Look on local universities' websites for the housing department's contact information to ask if they have housing available for students interning in the area. Student housing is often available for much less than normal rental prices in major metropolitan areas. For New York City specifically, StudentHousing.org lists a variety of university accommodation options for students.

HOSTELS

For those unfamiliar with hostels, they are establishments that provide inexpensive food and lodging for a specific group of people including travelers, workers, and students. Hostels are a terrific money saver when you travel internationally, and they can also be so during your internship. Many even offer private rooms and long-term stays. This is a considerably cheaper option than a hotel or renting an apartment. If you are a person who does well with communal living, a hostel might be just the right place for you.

FIND ROOMMATES

If you are interning in an area where university housing or hostels are not available, then your next best bet is to find a place with roommates. Sharing a space will dramatically reduce your bills compared to living by yourself. There are dozens of resources to help you find people you click with in your desired area. Websites such as RoommateFinders.com or even Craigslist.org can help students find affordable living situations in a pinch. Be smart when using these websites, though. Make sure to set up interviews with your potential roommates before you pay a deposit or agree to any financial commitments; also, do not be afraid to ask for references. Even if you cannot meet in person, set up a Skype chat to help determine if it will be a good fit.

Do not forget about your own network when looking for a room. Post on social media that you are looking for housing and/or roommates. Your friends and family may surprise you with resources you never knew about had you not asked. Also be sure to ask your classmates. Chances are they are looking to intern as well, and you can potentially live together. In addition, you can come home at the end of each day and share experiences as well as resources.

MONEY, MONEY, MONEY, MONEY! (I NEED MORE OF IT!)

So you don't have a paid internship. Don't worry! You can still pick up a part-time or other flexible job to bring in some cash to support yourself. What do you do to augment your income when you are taking classes? Take that same thought and apply it to the time you are interning. There are also many organizations that provide scholarships or grants to students that can be used for living expenses while interning. Similarly, it is important to know how to budget when you are living on a limited income, and the following tips can help you stretch a small amount of cash a long way.

PART-TIME JOBS

I have known many students over the years who interned during the day and then took on waiting tables or other night shift work to pay their bills. It is important that your side job is flexible so you can be present during the required hours of your internship. Do not fret though. Many companies with internship programs understand the financial pressures on students, and they are willing to work with you to create a schedule that works for you both. Of course you need to communicate and be upfront about your situation, but you can work it out.

The jobs that fit best with internships are often those with weekend or evening hours, like restaurant or bartending work. Some students have luck finding retail jobs on weekends or online positions that allow them to work outside of their intern hours by reporting remotely. Balancing two jobs can be very stressful, but if you can manage it (and I have faith that you can!), you will learn time management and how to work under pressure. Those skills become invaluable when applying for future positions as well as in general for the rest of your life.

Also, do not discount finding work within your field, even if on a peripheral level. For example, if you want to work in the music industry and you are looking at waiting tables or bartending, see if you can do so at a venue. Although those jobs are competitive, the fact that you are spending your days at a music company can help. Reminder: Every industry is interconnected. The person you are applying to work with at a venue may know your internship boss. It never hurts to ask in this situation because it is a very small world within each industry.

At the same time, the newly emerging "gig" economy whereby you choose which hours you work is a significant development for interns. Have a marketable skill? Put it up on Thumbtack.com. Willing to help with a chore or an errand? Sign up for TaskRabbit.com. Have a car and a license? Check out Lyft and Uber. Every day there are more and more start-ups offering hourly wages in which you can choose when you work, keeping your paid work schedule flexible. Jobs in the gig economy are perfect for students who need flexible schedules while they are studying or interning.

SCHOLARSHIPS & GRANTS

I knew that if I wanted to go to a private school in Boston and earn the degree of my dreams, I would need financial assistance to do so. Hence I worked extremely hard at swimming to earn the scholarship I needed. You can do the same for your internship. Make a list of all the organizations you or your family belong to, whether they are community or religious affiliations. There are also many scholarships available for students based on ethnicity, gender, heritage, and location.

FastWeb.com is a popular scholarship search engine that can help you find different organizations that award grants to active students. College Board is also a great resource to help you find grants and scholarships for which you may qualify. There are many sources out there, and a simple Google search of your activities or affiliations can reveal a wealth of information on potential funding.

Applying for these programs takes advance planning and often requires writing essays and gathering recommendations. If you are planning to apply for these scholarships and grants, you need to begin well ahead of your internship to make sure you have time to gather the relevant documents. If you are hoping to secure an internship for the summer, you should apply for scholarships in the fall semester or, at the very latest, early spring semester of your school year.

To that point, it's extremely important to plan ahead: You need to decide where you want to intern. Know that you will have far less competition if you are able to intern in the fall or winter, as most students intern in the summer. Do not be discouraged if summer is your only option, but keep an open mind to interning during the school year and taking classes during the summer. You may even enjoy the reduced campus population in the summer for some well-deserved peace and quiet after your busy semester interning in the "real world."

BUDGETING: LIVING ON A SHOESTRING AND A PRAYER

One of the key challenges of living in an expensive city is learning how to manage your money responsibly, which of course is a great life lesson as well. There are some very simple practices that can make a big difference when you are trying to save money. I have compiled a few tips that were helpful when I was counting change in New York as an intern.

1. **Make Your Own Meals.** If you have a kitchen in your living space, you can save tremendously by making your own breakfast, lunch, and dinner. Buying groceries is much cheaper than purchasing meals at a restaurant every day, and there are so many inexpensive meals that are nutritious and easy to make.

    Bringing your lunch to work will save you vast amounts of time and money. This is something I still do to this day, including when traveling for business. In addition to the financial incentive, bringing food from home provides a much healthier option than restaurant food, because you have total control over the ingredients you use. (Truth be told I still live this way as I love having kitchens whenever possible on business trips. It saves so much time to eat meals at my lodging that aren't otherwise happening during meetings.) We will discuss the benefits of good health on your career in Chapter 10. But suffice it to say when you are healthy, you perform better both at internships and at school, which will help you get ahead as well as potentially enjoy your life more.

2. **Eat Cheap.** If you do find you have to eat out, there are ways and places to dine on a budget. Do not order steak or large meat dishes; rather, look for economical items on the menu like salads, pastas, or hearty appetizers. In New York City you can find $2 pizza places that hit the spot and keep you filled up all day, while other cities have food trucks or diners serving affordable meals that will not break the bank.

3. **Drop the Starbucks.** If you are making your own meals, you should also get used to homemade or office coffee. That fancy latte you enjoy from Starbucks is $4+ each day. That quickly adds up to $20/week—by the end of your internship that could end up being over $200. A daily coffee may not seem like much at the purchase point, but it makes a big difference to your budget's bottom line when you are not earning a paycheck from your internship. The same goes for tea and water drinkers. A store-bought box of tea can cost the same as the amount many coffee shops charge for a single cup. And be sure to carry a water bottle with you; it is better for the environment than bottled water and you will feel good when you stay hydrated throughout the day.

4. **Cut Coupons.** It may seem like an old person thing to do, but grabbing a newspaper and spending a little time clipping coupons before you shop for your daily needs can really add up to some savings. This will make your grocery shopping a little more reasonable and help you reduce your food bills. Same for rewards programs in any form—you will be surprised at how quickly they add up to free goods or discounted rates both online and off.

5. **Walk When You Can.** If you are able to find housing within walking distance of your work, then you have scored major points in

the money-saving game. Walking to the Viacom/MTV building in Times Square when I interned at VH1 Classic (as well as running intern errands) enabled me to get to know New York City, which is knowledge that is still valuable to this day. Of course, many students are not able to land housing near their internship, so it is important to become familiar with your public transportation options. Avoid taking cabs, Uber, or Lyft because they can put a dent in your wallet. Walking more places saves you money, and it helps you maintain a healthy lifestyle.

But, there may come a time when you should not walk. I often attended late-night concerts and other music events, and walking home was not an option. Research helpful volunteer organizations such as RightRides. They ensure women get home safely late at night to the extent that they wait to make sure you are inside your building before driving away.

Beyond that, if you do need to take a taxi, see if you can split the cost with your fellow interns. And keep an eye out for Lyft and Uber promo codes. Definitely ask your supervisor at an appropriate time if ground transportation is covered when attending work or events past traditional office hours (very often it is). Bring this up in advance of the event, and even if it is not covered, I strongly encourage you to attend regardless. Remember that these experiences are building your network, career, and reputation. You owe it to yourself to see it through if you can.

If you implement these basic steps and secure additional income similar to what you may already be doing during the school year, then you are well on your way to making an unpaid internship affordable while simultaneously learning to master additional life and work lessons.

HOW NOT TO FEEL TAKEN ADVANTAGE OF
At the end of the day, once you have obtained the skills, the know-how, and the necessary contacts in your field, you will be paid as a skilled worker. Money is important. We need it to live.

That said, as an intern, if you feel you are being taken advantage of in regard to what you are contributing, ask someone experienced in the field about it to gain perspective. Ideally this should be someone outside of the company you are interning for. You may think you're being given disposable tasks that the company does not even need done in the first place, but in reality your efforts help to connect the work and projects for the folks you are interning for. If you are doing what you view as menial tasks, know that there is much to learn because these tasks ultimately plug into the bigger picture of the company. Imagine Lego or building blocks in your mind. Every piece is crucial and important, down to the envelope you correctly address.

Back in the day, I was thrilled to get paid to attend a concert and sell merch for Ed's band. That was my compensated paid gig. My career path escalated and led to other paying gigs when I interned for The Dresden Dolls while I was in college. I asked if I could tour manage the band. I did not ask to be paid on that first tour, and the band did not have much money at the time. But we ate well, and when the band went shopping for stage clothes, they bought me dresses. When they booked massages once in a while after their shows, they also included me. At the end of the tour, the band did end up paying me. Something I did not expect, and is a gesture that I am still grateful for.

That said, let me be clear: Whether you are touring (as I did) or in the office, *do not* pay for anything out of your own pocket. When I offered to tour manage The Dresden Dolls while in college, it was understood without question on both sides that they would cover my travel, lodging, and food expenses. I was horrified recently when an excited intern told me a band had offered to "let" her drive them around the country, tour manage, and sell merch, but she would have to foot the bill to fly back east when the tour ended in California.

This practice is unacceptable and not standard in the music industry. No gig is ever worth you having to pay for the privilege of doing work. It is one thing to gain experience and garner all of the benefits of interning without being remunerated; it is a completely different situation to pay for a businesses' expenses out of your pocket. The previously mentioned scenario is an example of an employer taking advantage of an intern.

The same goes for office expenses. Please do not pay for anything in advance, even if you know you will be reimbursed. Any professional company will provide you with funds in advance for approved expenses or for running errands that you are asked to do. Always save the receipts and give the change or credit card back to the person who gave you this responsibility.

As the business world moves to more cashless systems every day, do not forget to return the plastic! We have had numerous interns accidently walk off with cards. Intention aside, this can be inconvenient when the intern is not in every day and the company needs to use the card. Of course interns can also come back and return cards, but the easier route is to be on top of returning company cards as soon as the errand is completed. Similarly, do not pay for anything *assuming* you will be reimbursed if you have not been asked to do so.

Back to my first experience of tour managing The Dresden Dolls. Beyond that first tour and the wealth of experience I gained, not to mention The Dolls getting me my first stint running events at South by Southwest in Austin, Texas, the band and I continued to grow professionally together.

I worked hard and was very passionate about helping them succeed. This ultimately led to the band offering me a job once I graduated from college. A dream job that pays well right out of college is most likely the biggest short-term goal in your career—and I am living proof that it can be achieved. In the following chapters, I will continue to lay out the steps on how to significantly increase your chances of reaching this goal.

KEY TAKEAWAYS

Do an internship even if you think you can't afford it. You are going to need the real-world experience—not to mention the connections—that an internship provides, so be sure to set aside time and resources to commit to one or more internship opportunity. Think of an internship as just another part of college and factor it into your life accordingly. With some research and planning, you can make it work.

Create a budget and live by it. Even in expensive cities, you will save money by curtailing your spending. Give up luxuries like eating out, buying fancy coffee drinks, or taking cabs everywhere. It's also a great idea to use coupons, bring your lunch to work, and walk whenever possible rather than paying for transit.

Find a flexible gig to pay the bills. Shift work is great for people who need to work evenings and weekends so your days are free for interning. Consider bartending, waiting tables, tutoring, or babysitting as possible options. And don't forget the "gig" economy in which you can choose your own hours around your interning and school schedule.

Develop your networks at work. While your internship may not always pay you, realize that simply by *being there*, fully engaged, and learning all you can, you are getting to know leaders in your desired field and developing relationships that can take you far over time. Today, more than ever, it really is who you know—so put in the most amount of effort you can with what you're given to do and foster genuine connections that will prove valuable later.

Keep resentment and envy in check. Keep in mind that nearly anyone with a great position had to earn it, so try very hard not to resent others. And don't forget, those who haven't "paid their dues" get discovered and miss out on opportunities because of their inexperience. Instead of being envious, choose to be inspired, and let that passion inform your work. And from a practical standpoint, ask folks how they got to where you want to be; their answers may surprise you.

Work on your mindset. You need to get your head in the right place regarding unpaid internships. Your internship is an opportunity to try out any career to see if it is right for you, a chance to begin forging your future. Don't sweat the lack of cash—if you work hard now, you will develop the skills you need to have the career that you want – which is exactly the point of interning.

Three

How to Get an Internship

Research, Apply, and Nail the Interview.

I recently had the privilege of speaking at Juilliard on professional career development. Whether or not one wants to enter the performing arts space, I think we can all agree that Juilliard is one of the most prestigious and competitive schools in the world. Due to that, I was surprised when a Juilliard student asked how she should go about getting an internship. When I presented information on this topic, I watched the student and her classmates furiously take notes. So if you are feeling overwhelmed by this process, you are certainly not alone.

TO FIND YOUR DREAM JOB, START BY FOLLOWING YOUR PASSION

First, think about what you want to do within your specific field. If that is too daunting (as it was for me as an undergraduate), spend some time deducing what field(s) are of interest to you. Job security and money are also important factors, but ultimately it has been my experience that you're going to be most content in life by doing work that you like. For better or worse particularly in American culture, you are going to spend the vast majority of your days working. One might as well be spending this time working on projects which they feel passionate about and believe to be important.

There are a lot of facts in this book. The following, is an opinion. Mine was one of the first generations to be told: Do what you love. The answer to this from my young teenage self was "MUSIC!" I have zero regrets on my career and nothing would have stopped me from pursuing this path. During a recent conversation with a friend who has a young son, I blew her mind by taking this advice a step further; I said: "Do what you love that helps others." If you are lost or feeling overwhelmed about what field you should be pursuing, maybe this added insight will help shed some light onto your journey.

When I embarked on my internships at the age of 19, it was music, music, music. Yet I was concerned that I didn't know exactly what I wanted to do within the music industry. By following my own rule of never repeating an internship to enhance and maximize experience in my chosen field, I forged a strong background which has enabled me to become a respected artist manager and trusted advisor. I knew I loved music and wanted to help the source of this incredible art form in every way possible (artists). I also loved live shows, a passion that led me to my first job out of college as a tour manager.

An artist manager's job is to work with all facets of the music and entertainment industry cohesively to benefit the artist's short- and long-term career goals. Because I had acquired relevant experience working as an intern everywhere from a label to a radio station to television and beyond, I was able to understand what it was like for my colleagues working in various positions across the industry. This insight has made me a more empathetic businessperson, which ultimately has strengthened my reputation to the benefit of the artists whom I've represented, as well as my own career.

My point? If you don't know exactly what you want to do within your field, do not stress. The next steps will evolve naturally, even if they are not immediately apparent. Also, ask around. I guarantee you that colleagues, classmates, family members, and friends have all gone through something similar at one time or another.

If you're overwhelmed by which field to choose, a modern but very real problem for many, pick one to test the waters. A benefit of interning is to not only figure out what you want to do, but also to learn what you don't want to do. So start narrowing down your choices by interning. You'll be amazed at the clarity this provides.

PACK YOUR BAGS: INTERNSHIPS CAN TAKE YOU FAR AND WIDE

Once you have identified your field and/or some areas within your field that you want to try, start to figure out where these opportunities are based. As many internships are based in cities and my background is in entertainment, we're going to use major cities as the prime examples.

It's a cliché, but if you can make it in New York, you can generally make it anywhere. I personally love New York and have been told that I have the "energy" for it. If you have always wanted to live in and experience New York, I encourage you to try it. You can always go back to wherever you were before and there's nothing wrong with that as the city isn't for everyone.

That said, I feel living in New York is a great experience for any human who is drawn to try it, and that certainly isn't for everyone. My longtime business partner is based in Los Angeles and is the one who first said I have the "energy" for New York.

It's a generalization, but California does tend to be a bit more laid back. In L.A., you'll most likely need a car, though I know some who have survived successfully without one. If you're headed to San Francisco, my brother has commuted for years in the Bay Area on his bike. Regardless, whether you're in Chicago, Nashville, Seattle, or interning on a farm, many of the resources discussed in this book are applicable in just about every major city, both in the U.S. and abroad.

If you have an idea of where you will most thrive within your chosen field, start researching where you would like to intern. Keep the "where" in the back of your mind so you can start working on logistics shortly after you begin applying, as there is no need to put a deposit down on an apartment before you have landed your internship.

In general, take everything one step at a time. Working methodically will ensure you get everything done and also calm you down when you're feeling overwhelmed by having so much to do. (Taking healthy breaks in order to meditate, exercise, or hang out with friends, family and/or a pet can accomplish this as well.)

APPLYING FOR AN INTERNSHIP: THE ESSENTIAL STEPS

CHOOSE YOUR TARGET COMPANIES

If you are truly starting from scratch without any internship resources from your school, I recommend targeting five to twelve companies. I realize twelve potential internships is a lot—and you do want to focus in on what you want—but again, if you're undergoing this process on your own, make a list of your top five, with seven backups. It is important to be ambitious *and* well-prepared.

RESEARCH AND THEN RESEARCH SOME MORE

Then, do your research. Research your target company's website and social media. Google it in every way possible and read anything you come across. If the company is large enough, check out Glassdoor.com for real human reviews from folks who have worked there.

If there isn't much action on the company's social media pages, or there aren't social media pages at all (which may not be necessary if it's not a consumer facing company), maybe that's something you can help with or help start once you land your internship. We will discuss this further in Chapter 8 on how to best approach an idea you have for the company to ensure you are not overstepping any boundaries and come across in the best light possible.

Be mindful of when you are applying. For a January start date, apply in the fall. For a June start date, apply in Q1 ("Q1" is the first quarter of the year; January - March). Applying in January might result in a response to follow up in a few months. March is most likely the sweet spot but is also a busy time. February is your safest bet for the summer. Apply in May or June for a fall start date.

WRITE A RELEVANT RÉSUMÉ

Before you start applying, make sure your résumé is up to date. Again, don't fear putting down jobs you had in high school. If you dealt with people or did grunt work, I care! Many employers may not, but showing any sort of leadership on a résumé whether via a job or volunteer work will stand out across the board.

Any work you have done within the field helps as well. I had a colleague at a tech start-up focused on sports constantly frustrated with internship applicants expressing little if any interest in sports and/or tech. She was confused as to why some students were applying. At the same time, highlight your Twitter account and LinkedIn if appropriate to your field.

Does your résumé need a snail mail address? Probably not. I still see it pop up on résumés and always wonder why (most likely because schools still include this detail on their templates in prep classes). Of course don't put your résumé on, say, a neon background. At the same time, what your résumé looks like will help to influence whether or not people will read it. Keep it simple, clean (with regard to formatting), and to the point. Humans naturally skim when there are a lot of words, so be sure to keep your text concise.

Don't freak out too much if you don't have a "real" job to put on your résumé. Have you been a babysitter for years? Put it down. That's a job that requires responsibility, decision making, problem solving, leadership skills, time management, and multitasking. If you participate(d) in school clubs or extracurricular activities, list them—especially if you held leadership positions.

If you don't have these experiences, it's time to start getting involved! Volunteering on street teams or other local music promotion is great to mention when you're first putting together a résumé if you are, for example, pursuing a career in the music industry. At the same time, maybe the person you're interviewing with shares one or any of your extracurricular interests.

You never know; every little bit of information helps and gives you something viable to talk about during your interviews and in general with your potential colleagues. I had an intern apply recently who had done an intensive yoga teacher training in India. I think he was surprised that's what I wanted to hear about first, for a good 15 minutes or so. This was mostly out of self-interest as I love yoga, but it piqued my interest regardless.

Another item that stands out to me on résumés is if the student is multilingual or has spent any time abroad. Spending time in other countries in any form cranks your mind to work and think in a different and critical way.

> I'll never forget the challenge of figuring out how to buy a bus ticket in London. Seemingly simple day-to-day tasks such as that led me to problem-solving skills in my life and career. If I've tried to figure something out from every angle and still can't get it, I'll ask. But I figured out the bus, which taught my brain to at least try and solve the problem myself before asking, which has greatly expanded my brain over my lifetime. It sounds basic, but is true. Figuring out how to take the subway in Paris or Tokyo for a native English speaker is a simple but real challenge that helps to improve one's problem-solving skills.

I had an assistant whose dream job came up at another company. It's really important to me for the folks I work with to go after what they want with regard to career development. I not only told my assistant about it, but helped her try and get the gig. Although she was great, I could always hire another assistant; how often does one's dream job come up?

During that time, I happened to see her résumé, which was incredible. Usually résumés are boring and text driven. Although you don't necessarily want it to be in an outlandish font by any means, what stood out was the fact that she highlighted her personal social media accounts at the top of her résumé.

In a world where students are taught not to post photos of themselves drinking at parties on the Internet, this person went out of her way to showcase her social media because she had a clear love of music that was heavily present on her Twitter and Facebook accounts.

The colleague who interviewed her was equally impressed as it was not only clear that she had nothing to hide, but was an active participant at live shows and in the music industry—both of which were relevant to the hiring company. We will discuss developing a strong and genuine personal brand both online and off in Chapter 9. This story is a good example of how to help yourself stand out in ways that are advantageous.

CONQUER THE NEW "COVER LETTER" FOR THE MODERN ERA

Each field is different, so take this piece of advice with the specifics of your career area in mind. I think cover letters are dead. If you are applying for a finance or law job, it may still very well be applicable.

Ask around and use common sense with regard to where you are applying. If you have questions on how to format your résumé, most editing programs like Microsoft Word and Pages as well as Google Drive (which is free), have templates for you to use to begin building your résumé. Your college career services office undoubtedly will have a guide as well. If your school doesn't offer such services, websites such as CareerOneStop. org have several useful examples. A Google search will also yield countless examples tailored to your field.

In my world, the email you send with your PDF résumé attached *is* the cover letter. (Make sure the résumé is a reasonably sized attachment, i.e., under 5 MB so as not to clog your potential employer's inbox.) Because the "cover letter" is in email form, keep it short and to the point!

I receive hundreds of messages a day. Long ones are generally pointless, no matter who they are from. It may sound ridiculous but it's a waste of time if I have to click and open attachments just to read a cover letter. Put it in the body of the email; let's get to the point. Sending a résumé as a PDF attachment is totally fine, as mentioned, along with the email "cover letter" in the email's body.

We will discuss email etiquette in Chapter 5, but here are the basics: when applying, keep the email simple and straightforward. Mention **why** you'd like to intern at the company, and, if possible, say something specific about **why** you want to intern for the staff at that particular company.

An email from a student saying they are impressed with how I have developed our artists or a trade article I've written is going to go way further than "To Whom It May Concern, I'm interested in working in entertainment."

Amazingly, this is not entirely due to one's ego (though may be the case in many instances, which is fine!). We're trying to get your foot in the door here, so just ensure whatever you say is genuine. When a student mentions particulars on why they want to join a company, it conveys they have taken the time to research the company and therefore may fit into the company's culture and ethos. Here is an example with regard to length and content:

Subject: January Internship

Dear Emily, (Ms. White is fine, but I'm going to correct you really quickly that formalities are not necessary in the entertainment industry.)

I am a music industry major at X University. As an avid reader of Hypebot *(a trade journal in our field), I have gleaned a lot of information from your articles on the modern music business over the years.*

Similarly, I am impressed with how you have applied these tactics to your roster at Whitesmith Entertainment in terms of advising artists who all clearly have specific career goals.

I am applying for internships beginning in January and have attached my résumé if you are taking interns on at that time. I'd be happy to help with your sports and comedy divisions if that is useful to the company as well.

Please don't hesitate to contact me if you need anything from me, including references.

Thanks so much,
Name
Best contact phone number

The email above clearly states where the student goes to school and what they are studying; it also conveys they are passionate about the business end of the field since they regularly read at least one key industry trade journal and have spent time researching our company. The email also shows that the prospective intern knows we work in more than music and that they want to make an impact in every way possible.

Offering references up front is helpful as well as it shows you are already building a reliable and positive reputation. I can read an email like this quickly and know exactly what it's all about. The text is clear and to the point and assuming we set up a phone interview, their phone number is right there for my assistant, A.I., or I to add into my calendar for when the interview time comes. (It's not the best use of our time to send unnecessary emails asking for this information, which seems trivial, but our time is very limited.)

Even if you're dying to add more to the email, it's going to hurt you. Put that information in your résumé and save other details for your interview. By keeping it simple and straightforward, you have a better shot of landing an interview. Also, you will have more to say during the interview. If you tell your life story out of the gate, your email may not even be read in-full. It's not that we don't care about you or interns in general; it's that there are only so many hours in the day. Be mindful of that.

Our company's website offers an email address for internship inquiries. I leave it pretty general as I'm interested to see how students initially present themselves. The most professional students are invariably going to stand out from the get-go.

Many companies do not have any information posted on internships, and others may never have even thought of the concept. Why? They may be too busy! I truly believe it never hurts to ask, albeit respectfully. You may even create your own dream internship this way if internships where you want to work do not exist until you inquire and create one (which is what happened to me with The Dresden Dolls).

IF YOUR DREAM INTERNSHIP DOESN'T ALREADY EXIST, CREATE IT

As mentioned in the Chapter 1, my initial plan was to figure out a way to get my foot in the door at Ignition, the company that manages Oasis. What happened instead was that a great local band called The Dresden Dolls played at my school. When they played at Northeastern, I bought a few of their CDs for friends whom I thought would also like the band.

The band was doing quite well locally and was increasing in popularity. As they were doing so well, I was hesitant to ask whether they needed help, but when buying the CDs I introduced myself to the band's singer, Amanda Palmer. I let her know that I was a music industry major at the school, was interning at a local radio station, writing for a local music magazine, and would be happy to help if she ever needed anything. Her response: "Can you come over tomorrow?"

From my perspective the band was getting big. Why would they need my help? In reality, they were on the cusp of breaking with a small and homegrown team in place and very few traditional industry folks on board at the time.

It turned out that the band's frontwoman lived just a few minutes' walk from campus. I would head over every day after class and before swim practice to embark on an experience that would eventually change my life and career. **Inspired by my passion and determination, I created an internship that would otherwise not exist**.

It's the same in the traditional business world. I have worked at small and large companies that didn't have internship programs until I raised the issue. Figure out your dream gig and go for it—it truly never hurts to ask in this area.

A WORD ON APPLYING FOR THE "IT" INTERNSHIP

That said, what if you're applying at hotly sought-after internships, such as Google, that are rife with competition? Again, do your research, immerse yourself in the tech field, and follow all of the above steps while soaking up information on previous interns who have posted about their experiences online. And don't be deterred.

I always thought it would be amazing to intern with *The Late Show with David Letterman.* I applied every summer and never heard back. Apply at other start-ups that you are interested in. On the one hand, you might land at the next Uber, Facebook, or Apple. On the other, you'll be getting experience on the ground floor, which is universally invaluable to your career whether the company succeeds or not.

A FEW THINGS TO KEEP IN MIND BEFORE YOU HIT "SEND"

Once you've narrowed down your target list, have your résumé ready to go, and ensure that your social media accounts look professional, it's time to start applying.

In my world, I would rarely "pitch" to someone on a Monday morning. That said, I think sending your résumé on a Monday or Tuesday in the late morning is the way to go. In a professional setting, most folks are digging out on Mondays and aren't quite alert yet from the weekend.

Responding to an internship applicant is pretty easy and is mindless work that can be done quickly on a Monday instead of more complex projects (no offense). I'm fine with applying on a Wednesday late morning, but don't push it too much further after that. People are exhausted by Thursday, and by Friday they are ready for the weekend.

Additionally, avoid sending your application on a holiday and the day following the holiday. Always try to put yourself in the shoes of the person who will be receiving your application as the aforementioned days are always busy. Keep these "day of the week" tips in mind in general throughout your career. It's not just intern pitches that shouldn't happen on holidays, weekends, or late in the week. Use these tips to increase your chances of obtaining a response with work correspondence in general.

> *Here's another tip: follow the company on Twitter and Instagram and "like" them on Facebook. This shows that you are interested in what the company is doing. For larger companies that are unlikely to notice such gestures, you'll at least be in the loop with what they are doing publicly. Re-tweet and share things that the company is doing that are important and of interest to you. Perhaps do this once or twice while you're applying and interviewing, and do so whenever you are inspired to once you have the internship. This will continue to show the people involved in the company's social media that you care while simultaneously expanding your online network.*

YOU'VE APPLIED FOR THE GIG…NOW WHAT?

I truly believe that if you follow these steps and apply to five to twelve companies of various sizes the semester before you want to intern, you're going to get at least one response. If you don't receive a response within two weeks, call all of the companies you applied to. Hopefully you will encounter someone friendly on the phone. Respectfully let them know that you applied for an internship two weeks ago via email and wanted to know if that is the best way to get in touch before you followed up via email. Hopefully the person asks you to re-forward the email in case it went into spam. Better yet if that person happens to be the intern supervisor, as you now have reinforced yourself for name recognition amongst a sea of emails.

If you do not receive any responses within two weeks, apply to another five companies to expand your list. Also, ask around. Post on your Facebook page. I recently brought on an intern from my hometown who posted on Facebook that his dream was to tour manage bands. It turns out that one of his friends was a high school swimming teammate of mine and he's now learning the ropes, helping members of Wilco, a.k.a. The Autumn Defense, to prepare for a festival in a few months.

You're building your network from day one, and your classmates may know of internships they completed and can introduce you to someone. Same for your professors. Personal touches go a long way. If a friend or family member can make an introduction, that's great as well. But as a reminder, it's on you after that. Which is what this book is all about.

PREPARING FOR YOUR INTERVIEWS

Hopefully at this point, you've landed at least one interview. Of course you want to be accommodating to the company's schedule, but bearing that in mind, and assuming you are applying in a different city, it's not at all out of line to let the interviewer know when you are available to be in their city. That said, do not offer yourself up for weekends and after hours. It is inconsiderate to the interviewer's time and shows that you do not have an understanding of general business hours and etiquette.

I want people to go above and beyond of course, but also to demonstrate they have work-life balance. I often do phone interviews to help save time, but many companies will offer in-person interviews depending on the nature of the internship. As a college student I would take the $10 Chinatown bus in between Boston and New York, oftentimes going to and from NYC in a day to save on lodging costs when attending internship interviews.

CHOOSE THE RIGHT ATTIRE FOR YOUR FIELD

Once you have landed your interview, you need to consider what to wear! Ask around if you are unfamiliar with the dress code of your field. I don't know many industries in this day and age that require a full business suit, but they of course do exist.

The entertainment and tech industries tend to be more laid back. So while you don't want to show up with stains on your t-shirt (and frankly, if you spill coffee on yourself right before you walk in, explain that in a funny way as it'll humanize you), I recommend looking like you put some effort in, but not trying too hard. Smart/business casual is the way to go in the fields of entertainment and tech.

During the first year of my management company, I'll never forget when an 18-year-old intern applicant named Dan showed up to my apartment for an interview (I worked from home at the time) in a dress shirt and tie! Poor thing.

We of course didn't hold it against him and he went on to do great things, eventually founding the successful blog and website Allston Pudding. Networking side note: Dan was introduced to me by an ex-boyfriend who told me I *had* to listen to The Dresden Dolls. It's a small, small world, but more on networking in Chapter 9.

ARRIVE JUST BEFORE YOU'RE DUE

When do you show up for your interview? My colleague Caryn Rose of *Billboard* recently tweeted: "PLEASE do not show up 15 minutes before an interview unless instructed to. Five is plenty. Hang at Starbucks."

As I arrived 30 minutes early for my interview with Bob Ezrin, who produced Pink Floyd's *The Wall* in addition to a slew of other legendary albums, I found some steps a block away and sat quietly reviewing my career achievements and answering questions in my head I thought he might ask.

Of course you want to give yourself plenty of time to get to the interview location, leave time to get lost, and have some extra taxi money on hand if you get confused about the directions. And if you do take a taxi in New York—know the cross streets! No one will know the location of an address if that's what you give them (which I did the first time I ever gave a taxi a location). If you have a smartphone, you can also look up the cross streets by typing the address into Google Maps. More on this later, but Google Maps is your friend! Do not ask supervisors for directions if you have a smartphone as they will wonder why you aren't utilizing that. Get familiar with Google Maps in advance of your internship if you aren't already.

FIND YOUR CENTER AND GO FOR IT

I'm a particular brand of freak as I used to like internship and job interviews (once I got through my first few). The interview is all about you, so I didn't find it difficult to answer questions about myself. Be yourself, be genuine, and take a deep breath to help with your confidence.

To this day I think it is very important to exercise every day, let alone before an interview or speaking engagement. Yoga in particular helps with posture and poise, which I've had people comment on positively when I'm doing on-camera or live speaking engagements. I always credit yoga for my posture. Meditating before an interview (which can be done anywhere, including at a café or even a bathroom), can also help to focus your mind before an interview while simultaneously settling your diction into a natural rhythm.

ACING THE INTERVIEW: PRACTICAL TIPS TO HELP YOU CONNECT, IMPRESS, AND CLOSE

A firm but reasonable handshake is appropriate when meeting the interviewer. To this day when opening business exchanges, I always ask, "How has your morning (or) day been going so far?" People rarely take the time to care and ask such a question, and it's a good ice breaker whether you're an intern or executive.

If the interviewer doesn't take the lead for some reason, a great follow-up question (which can also be used towards the end of the interview), is to ask where the person interviewing you is from. Who knows, maybe you're both from the same state/region, like I was with Winifred during my first interview. All human connections will help you.

Bring at least two hard copies of your résumé. I'm stunned when people show up without their résumé as I do not often have the time (or even the resources if I'm on the go) to print one and this is super helpful. Though I've been equally impressed when an intern interviewee who didn't have a hard copy instantly problem solved and pulled it up on her device. At the same time, it's easier for me to reference a piece of paper while interviewing you in person, so please bring your résumé, which will also show that you are thoughtful and polite. As even if you've emailed your résumé to us, it's one of many messages we receive and we appreciate the ease of applicants handing us their résumé to keep things moving and streamlined.

If you are doing a phone interview—**do not** talk over the interviewer! This happens to me from time to time and blows my mind. I'd love to chalk it up to nervousness, but often get the vibe that it's arrogance.

One student recently rambled on about his current internship at Powderfinger, which happened to be my first internship. He mentioned something about the boss that seemed odd and then said, "But he's cool, he has a photo with David Bowie hung up in the office." I said, "Is it a group photo?" He said, "Yes." I said, "I'm in that photo and arranged the entire meeting with Bowie while I was an intern there." (Bowie had done a meet & greet with WBCN and I invited Winifred along, thus the photo.)

I was surprised that this intern applicant was not only talking over me, but didn't do any research to find out that I had interned there and also knew his boss quite well (the latter often being an easy thing to look up via Facebook and LinkedIn connections). This is of course not required information, but will help you stand out if you know something about the person you're interviewing with. Also, it doesn't take long. While I am not famous and have a common name, there is a *ton* of information about my career all over the Internet in relatively concise forms.

Knowing some background information about the person who is interviewing you will help show that you are prepared, and it saves me having to explain basic information that is easily accessible online. You don't want to stalk the person, but if you're from Wisconsin and have stumbled on the fact that I am, mention that. Did you swim or play another sport in college? Do you share my love of Britpop? Tell me! If we have nothing in common publicly, don't sweat it! Relax, be yourself, and your interest and passion will hopefully shine through in a respectful way when any or all of the previous tips have been followed.

Finally, choose an appropriate time to ask the interviewer the following: *How did you get your start, either at the company or within the field?* People love to talk about themselves and this will not only help the interviewer to engage with you, but you may also learn valuable knowledge that you can apply to your career. I believe this is one of the best questions to ask when you are asked if you "have any questions," which will invariably happen in every interview situation you are ever in.

Of course if you have practical questions, ask those too. But ultimately, you really want to kill it at your internship, which means the hours and type of work you do shouldn't matter. Make sure to mention if you have solid part-time paid work or are, say, training for a sport the way I was. Most internship bosses are understanding and will work with you on your schedule. They may even be interested in what you are doing. There are countless bosses and colleagues who found the fact that I was a scholarship swimmer to be incredibly interesting.

But don't ask about hours if it doesn't actually affect you. It can come off as sounding like you want to put in the minimal amount of time possible, whether that is the intention or not. The information will come, and if it's an 80-hour work week (which is illegal), you can deal with that when the time comes. Most internships are a few days a week during regular business hours. Which means showing up on time and working late if need be. But again, if you have previously discussed legitimate obligations, only a crazy person will have a problem with that. And, working for crazy people is generally not fun or healthy. Avoid it at every stage of your career if you can.

No matter how great you feel about your interview skills, definitely practice with a friend or family member a few times before you begin interviewing. Practicing your handshake and tackling mock questions can make a world of difference. It can also temper any nerves you may be experiencing.

One of the greatest lessons my attorney and dear friend Joyce Dollinger taught me is: "Prepare, prepare, prepare!" She couldn't be more right. Joyce gave me this advice before I spoke at my first major panel with folks such as the founder of Pandora. The prep I did with my friend made a world of difference and resulted in Tim Westergren (said founder of Pandora) tweeting that if he was in a band today, he'd want me to be his manager. I'm glad I practiced and prepped!

Finally, sending a short thank-you email the following <u>business</u> day is perfect. Example:

Dear Emily,

Thank you so much for taking the time out of your day to interview me. I really appreciate it! I'd be honored to intern at X Company if you are interested.

Please don't hesitate to contact me if you need any additional references or information.

Enjoy the rest of your week (or weekend)!

Take care,
Name
Best phone number to reach you

If you do all of the above, you will greatly increase your odds of landing your dream internship. Congrats! But also know that this is just the beginning.

KEY TAKEAWAYS

Follow your passion. If you're not sure which industry you'd like to work in, think carefully about what brings you the most joy. Start from this point and explore potential careers related to your passions. This should help you narrow the possibilities down to a few distinct fields. Also keep in mind that you will feel the most purpose when you find ways to help others through the work you do.

Research the companies you're interested in. The more you learn about the businesses you'd like to intern with, the better prepared you will be in general. Learn all you can about the staff and their notable accomplishments. This shows them that you've taken a genuine interest and will likely understand the company and its culture. Also be sure to follow the companies and key team members on social media.

Cast a wide net. It sounds extreme, but you want to apply to as many as twelve internships so you're more likely to gain at least a few interviews. When you have several responses, you'll feel accomplished and confident—which only helps you as you prepare for your upcoming meetings.

Put together a great application package. If you take the time to be thorough, organized, and add a bit of your own personal flair to your résumé and cover letter, it will definitely show and pay off for you. So pay attention to details and make sure your introductory email is genuine, specific, and concisely to the point.

Get comfortable with interviewing. When you are well prepared and at ease, an interview can be a great experience. Practice your interview skills from hello to goodbye with a friend to accustom you to being succinct, professional, and yourself when under pressure. Keep in mind that an interview is your time to shine! That said, take a deep breath before you head in for your interviews and remember that we're all human at the end of the day, no matter the title of the person interviewing you.

Four

Preparing for Your Internship

Understanding Your Industry and Pre-Internship Research to Get the Most Out of Your Experience(s).

ONCE YOU HAVE LANDED YOUR INTERNSHIP, NOW WHAT?

Before your internship begins, there's often an interim period in which you can further prepare for your upcoming role. It is important to use this valuable time wisely. Build on the research you began during your application process. Assuming you are already following the company and/or key players on Twitter/Instagram and have "liked" the company on Facebook, check these pages a few times a week to keep up to date with their news.

If the company offers any public events that are promoted on their social media, definitely attend if you can and absolutely introduce your-self to people. Certainly let your internship supervisor know in advance if you're attending as they will most likely be impressed; it will also mean you have someone to say hello to in person when you turn up. If this thought alone terrifies you, feel free to skip ahead to Chapter 9, which is all about networking.

IT'S RECON TIME: WHY YOU SHOULD IMMERSE YOURSELF IN YOUR NEW INDUSTRY

I can't stress the importance of this type of research enough. I am constantly surprised when students begin an internship with us and do not know the artists on our roster. Not that they are necessarily Beyoncé level, but it doesn't take much time (and this research should be fun and not painful) to get to know our clients' music, comedy, and accomplishments in advance—especially in a field where abbreviations are common. Therefore, if your first task is to research something for a client whose initials I use when communicating internally, hopefully you'll be familiar enough with the roster that you immediately understand to whom I'm referring.

Similarly, know your industry! If you're interning for, say, a basketball team, get to know the players' names on the team. Familiarize yourself with the other teams, players, and key industry folks and concepts in the league and entire industry.

Read industry blogs, news outlets, and websites (often referred to as B2B, short for "Business to Business," which means it is industry information, as opposed to a "Consumer Facing" outlet in which the general public is the intended audience). Hypebot.com, Billboard.biz, *Billboard*, *Rolling Stone*, and *Variety* are good places to start as far as music and entertainment trade publications go. Subscribe to these in your RSS reader of choice to not miss a beat.

> *You'll pick up a lot on how to stay informed in your industry at your internship, but no one is going to sit you down and necessarily train you on your field at large. I have to assume you have interest in the area you're interning in, so this should be second nature to some extent, but I've noticed it isn't always for a lot of folks. If the latter is you, dig in on this chapter to maximize results and expand the knowledge of your career choice beyond your specific internship.*

I can't stress enough how important it is to immerse yourself in your industry. Go to *every* event possible, even if it doesn't seem like the most interesting thing to do or is something you wouldn't otherwise check out. Say yes to everything you are invited to, and suddenly (rather, within a few years), you'll look back and have more knowledge and contacts than you know what to do with.

Remember: most jobs and fields are competitive. Although a balanced life is very important, know that there are others out there who are passionate about their careers as well. If you are not passionate, interested, and/or engaged regarding your work, it will be tough to break through.

Maybe that outward passion doesn't come naturally to you, so I point this out to ensure you're doing the necessary research to get ahead in your field. No one will be coming to you. You have to put yourself out there in each and every industry, which also requires undertaking online research, including social media.

GET CLEAR ON YOUR EXPECTATIONS FOR YOUR INTERNSHIPS

Before you begin your internship, it's hard not to imagine what it will be like. I try to make it very clear to prospective interns during interviews that if they are interested in getting into the entertainment industry because they think it entails being cool and hanging out, they should think again.

Artist management in particular, like most things, is *work*. It's *a ton* of emailing, phone calls, meetings, staying on top of schedules, keeping things organized, *and then* having enough energy to attend shows, undertake promotional work, and attend industry networking events. Ultimately a love and passion of the field should come first, but students need to be equally passionate about the work at hand to succeed in competitive fields.

People ask me from time to time what the most rewarding aspects of my work are. It's truly hard to say. On the one hand, it's of course incredible when you're at a successful event that you helped organize and maybe even thought of in the first place. I get just as excited when an email response comes in with great news for one of our artists based on something I pitched, or a schedule and logistical plan comes together that was all handled on my laptop and phone.

If you expect your career and internships to be pure fun, at least in the entertainment industry, I encourage you to stay a fan. If you know you're equally a geek about the work as much as you love the arts, then this is the field for you (this concept is the same from my perspective, no matter what the industry).

I mention all of this so you begin your internship with realistic expectations. I don't want to discourage you, as it's natural to be excited. As much as you want to prepare, it is beneficial to be a blank slate when it comes to thinking about the actual tasks you will be doing. The following chapters include the necessary information to complete common internship tasks successfully.

Ultimately, it's on you to take on and complete each task with professionalism and enthusiasm. If you're making copies, make sure the copies are organized perfectly and look great. If you're given literally nothing to do, observe what's going on around you.

Listen in on conversations around you respectfully. Take in and soak up the company's vibe and culture, as I guarantee you it's different from a school setting. These are all ways to maximize what otherwise may seem like menial tasks for your maximum benefit.

Don't necessarily expect excitement. People say to me all of the time that my job must be so "exciting." Yes, the travel and events look fun on my social media and is fun—but that "fun" requires *a lot* of planning to execute. I didn't get into music to spend most of the day on a laptop, but that is the reality of working in both the modern music industry as well as modern business, for better or worse right now.

In short, temper your expectations. Be excited, but don't expect to be given the lead on a major marketing project at your internship on day one. Take each step seriously, no matter what it is, and also think about how it plugs into the bigger picture of the company, because I guarantee you, it does.

I was heartbroken recently when an aspiring tour manager stated that she might "suck it up" and do merch (a.k.a., sell t-shirts, etc., at concerts) for a bit to get experience. I loved ensuring that The Dresden Dolls' merch table looked gorgeous and flawless, down to every t-shirt being perfectly folded, when I was an intern. Take ownership and pride in every task you are given, and I guarantee that you will learn, grow and that people will notice.

I love my life, don't get me wrong, but in hindsight I had way more fun when I was "coming up" in my career doing whatever was asked of me and doing it well. Those formative years were a blast, and I wouldn't trade them for anything. Be it as an intern or tour manager, those memories will last forever. My best friend is a professional merchandise person who is in high demand on major tours that pay well and take her around the world on a regular basis. We had a blast traveling the globe and working together in our 20's and I wouldn't have had it any other way.

STARTING AT THE BEGINNING: WHY EACH RUNG ON THE CAREER LADDER IS SO CRUCIAL

Ultimately, I blossomed in my field by *mastering*, not skipping, each step along the way. This has led to constant career growth, evolution, and success. I remember as a young tour manager (for The Dresden Dolls) just out of college on the Nine Inch Nails tour, being given some great advice by a lighting director on the tour.

Nine Inch Nails' production manager was incredibly intimidating, and clearly experienced and fantastic at his job. His role was to oversee and interact with every person on the large crew to ensure the band's very technical show went off without a hitch each night. This was also an arena production touring in oftentimes historic (and therefore old) theatres. It was a very cool experience for the fans to see a large band in smaller venues, but a daunting task for the team behind it.

After observing all of this, the lighting director said to me: "Do you know why Chris is so good at his job as production manager? Because he's done all of our jobs before." Chris didn't skip any steps along the way to being the person in charge of Nine Inch Nails' touring production. He had to work and master each skill along the way, only to rise to what is a major and ultimately very stressful job.

I think about this when I look back on my career. I used to view the music industry like a mountain that I was constantly climbing. After my name graced the cover of *Billboard* and it felt like just about everyone in the industry knew who I was, I felt like I had reached the peak to some extent. Looking around the summit, I thought, "This is it?" It seemed vastly empty. I realized that my experiences while climbing to the top were in many ways the most fruitful elements of my overall career.

It's not that I don't love my job now—but it's a lot of pressure to be in charge and at "the top." You have many people relying on you, and even if that comes naturally, the gig is constant. It's an embarrassing lyric to admit, but I'm reminded of an Aerosmith line that states, "Life's a journey, not a destination" (which, in reality, is a Ralph Waldo Emerson quote, but ultimately I know it from loving *Get a Grip* in sixth grade).

This couldn't be more true for my career. There was almost more fun in making sure The Dresden Dolls' merchandise table was perfect, and running around the globe with amazing people in my twenties as a tour manager, than there is now. At the same time, I recently launched a new start-up as I always want to grow and learn, which shows that we never stop evolving.

I love my life, but when you are coming up, you will most likely have more time and passion for your field than ever. So although the future will unfold with exciting things, don't forget to enjoy your time now, even if the tasks seem menial. Similarly, I guarantee that you are learning as you go, whether you are making coffee, photocopying, or just soaking up the modern workplace environment.

THE LEGAL INS AND OUTS OF INTERNING

Before you begin your internship, it's important to understand what an internship is and what it isn't. An internship is an opportunity for you to get your foot in the door of your chosen field so you learn new skills, grow, and create a professional network before you graduate.

Incredibly busy companies and professionals are taking time out of their seemingly infinite work days to train you. Or maybe they don't train you! I promise there are benefits to either scenario and everything in between, which we'll discuss in Chapter 7.

Here are the six legal requirements for an unpaid internship as put forth by the U.S. Supreme Court:

1. The internship, even though it includes actual operation of the facilities of the employer, is similar to training which would be given in an educational environment.
2. The internship experience is for the benefit of the intern.
3. The intern does not displace regular employees, but works under close supervision of existing staff.
4. The employer that provides the training derives no immediate advantage from the activities of the intern; and on occasion its operations may actually be impeded.
5. The intern is not necessarily entitled to a job at the conclusion of the internship.
6. The employer and the intern understand that the intern is not entitled to wages for the time spent in the internship.

I would be remiss if I did not point out these legalities in this book. They are super important. Abuse of interns' time does happen. But if you are looking to sue an employer, this book isn't for you.

I am saddened and stunned by the countless internship lawsuits that are dominating the headlines. Most companies that are faced with a lawsuit eventually eliminate their internship programs. This in turn eliminates the opportunity for future interns to get their foot in the door of legendary companies, such as Condé Nast (home of *Vogue* and much more), Warner Music Group, The Agency Group (now United Talent Agency), as well as various film studios.

If you feel that you are being taken advantage of, speak with your school about it, a colleague outside of your company to get some perspective, or the human resources department if you are not a student. It has been my experience that if you do a great job, you will build a network and evolve into your career. This hard work may increase your chances of being in the "right place at the right time" when there is a job opening at your internship. **More often than not, it is the network you develop in and around your internship that will lead to a job.**

Similarly, staying in touch with colleagues you have created professional relationships with through your internship can help lead to jobs being passed along to you when the time comes. It would be impossible for us to hire every student that comes through our company, even just the top interns. I'm happy to pass along and make recommendations for job openings I know of to interns. In addition, colleagues come to me when looking to hire because I work with so many great students and spend time mentoring them.

WHY I WROTE *INTERNING 101*

Now we're going to evolve into the basis of this book and why it exists in the first place. Soak it all up, and get your highlighter, notepad, laptop, or whatever you need to learn every skill I'm about to outline.

The following is what was initially dubbed at my company as "The Intern Manifesto," which is ultimately the concept behind this book. I realized I was explaining modern business how-to's every semester, from the basic to the cerebral. I wrote "The Intern Manifesto" as our company's handbook that has become our interns' go-to reference point for basic information and guidelines. It's there for the interns to reference before they ask a supervisor.

When I realized that top students found it to be a useful tool, I asked some of our best interns if developing "The Intern Manifesto" into a book would be helpful to them and their classmates. The response? A collective "YES!" As a result, *Interning 101* was born. The rest of the book is an expanded version of "The Intern Manifesto" for my company's internal use.

Here we go!

KEY TAKEAWAYS

Learn as much as you can before you walk in the door. Do as much research as you can before beginning your internship. Read up on industry websites, and immerse yourself in learning about key industry figures and concepts. Additionally, follow your internship's company on social media and attend any appropriate events before your start date.

Manage expectations. Be prepared to work very hard before you achieve success. Many careers seem glamorous and fun, but also require extreme focus and tenacity. Keep this in mind as you're running errands and picking up lunch. You may not be promoted on day one, but trust that you are laying the groundwork and gaining experience for the future.

Enjoy the journey at every stage. It's important to try and find joy at every level of your career. Don't bemoan putting in the time and effort it takes to obtain knowledge and credibility in your field. Deliver your very best, whether you're folding t-shirts or attending a meeting with the staff. Everything you do is building your know-how, deepening your confidence, and will come in handy further down your path.

Be clear on what an internship is (and isn't!). An internship allows you to gain knowledge and skills needed to work in your chosen field. It is also a chance to expand your professional network. If you are feel you are being taken advantage of at your internship, ask your mentors to ensure all is in line. You more often than not may be reminded of the networking contacts you're gaining as well as the big picture goals you are working towards, one step and every day at a time.

Five

Modern Office Basics Part 1

Email 101, Slack, Asana, and Not Fearing the Phone.

Now down to the nitty-gritty basics for your internship! If you treat any chapters in this book as your Bible/Torah/Quran/Atheist's Guide (whichever is most appropriate for you!), I believe it should be this along with Chapter 6. Together, they will be handy as a reference while you're experiencing your actual internship(s).

In this chapter, we are going to break down all of the basic skills I believe interns should have to maximize their performance for supervisors, teams, and careers. Some of this information might be boring and second nature to you. If so, awesome! You have a leg up on your peers. If not, do not stress-out. The vast majority of schools currently do not teach this information. Therefore, this is not your fault and you are on par with your classmates. Albeit with a huge advantage with the knowledge contained within this book.

One of the most beneficial courses I have ever taken was called "Software Applications." I took this during my sophomore year of high school. The class taught us the basics of spreadsheets, word processing (a.k.a. Microsoft Excel and Word), as well as typing skills. To this day, I use the skills from that class to format everything from marketing one-sheets, to the draft of this book that I'm currently writing, to the basic formulas that power an Excel spreadsheet. (As you'll see, the concept of a stand-alone spreadsheet as an attachment is pretty much dead in the cloud/Google Drive/collaborative era, with the underlying concepts of spreadsheets remaining the same.) Let's get started.

The reason a working knowledge of these tools is so valuable is quite simple: they are the means by which your company tells you what they need from you. If you can't use them, you won't know—and if you don't know, you won't succeed. Interning for one of my companies is apparently like intern boot camp. About 25% of our interns unfortunately fail. The rest, who follow all instructions, work hard, and do everything that is asked of them, consequently thrive. They succeed and go on to do great things in life.

> It's really important in all levels of business to not take anything personally. People are often focused on themselves and what is going on in their lives. If a supervisor seems stressed, upset, or doesn't have much time to spend with you, it is more likely than not that this has nothing to do with you. I deeply care about each and every person I work with on a human level. Their health and happiness is the priority. Beyond that? I care about getting work done to our clients' and company's benefit.

That said, here is the opening of my company's Intern Manifesto:

> Please read this. It's important. Read everything we ever send you. With regard to emails, **always read threads from the bottom up**.

EMAIL: A NECESSARY "EVIL" IN TODAY'S WORKPLACE

No one loves email, but for most modern companies, it's not going away anytime soon.

As of this writing, Slack is making inroads toward overthrowing email, which is a very exciting development. A tech industry standard that is creeping into mainstream business as well, Slack is a great tool on a few levels, particularly to cut down on internal emails. At its core, Slack is a messaging system that allows companies to break into teams and projects for internal communication. The platform does much more than that, but for now, we'll focus on its internal messaging powers, how it saves time, and increases efficient communications.

That said, you will still need email skills for now to professionally communicate with external colleagues. Email is a largely important tool in my world for many reasons. For one, it makes people state what they are doing and, in theory, forces them to be accountable for certain tasks as there is a written record of this communication. On the internal front, many tasks have moved over to project management platforms such as Asana and Trello, which is great! When dealing with people outside of the company, it's still incredibly important to know how to communicate via email to get things done as efficiently as possible.

The proper use of email is a critical skill that most interns don't yet have. This is understandable when one thinks about it. Who have you really emailed in your life to date? Most likely your professors, your parents, and maybe your classmates. Until Slack came about, I was sending and receiving about 300 emails a day. Slack has helped to cut this down for sure, but knowing how to write a short, to the point, robust, and professional email is still a crucial skill for most people in all types of businesses.

To this day I have pretty much read every business email I've ever been sent from the bottom up. That way I can glean all information from the conversation, know who everyone is, and what they said.

I used to love reading emails from the bottom up when they were sent to me as an intern. This helped me begin to figure out who folks were in the industry, what they did, and how they communicated. It is an absolute must that you do the same. You can even search for people via Google for more on their career backgrounds and check out what they are saying on Twitter. They are most likely folks who work successfully in your field, which is exactly what you're aspiring to do. So use this tactic to get to know who people are, what they do, and how they communicate with each other.

Also, every field has certain industry terms that are almost always learned within the field. In the music industry, you need to become familiar with vocabulary such as: first hold, ticket count, ticket buy, song split, merch (as mentioned), rough mix, and mastering. There are countless terms like this in every area of business and the more you read real life communication chains from the bottom up, the more you'll know what people are talking about.

RESPOND TO EMAILS WITHIN 24 BUSINESS HOURS WHENEVER POSSIBLE

What happens when an email is written to you? For our company, we ask that interns reply to emails or internal messages within 24 business hours. If they can't get to an email or task, that is fine, they just need to **tell us.** As mentioned, this is where a significant amount of interns fail.

I understand that students are used to a world where they can miss a class or not turn in an assignment from time to time and still get by. Of course in the business world, we all make mistakes once in a while. However, if there is anything in my career I am confident and proud of, it is my reputation for reliability. Not only does one not have the luxury of skipping a task from time to time in the business world, it is to your benefit to complete all tasks to the absolute best of your ability for your own reputation's benefit.

If you are unable to do something, it is more professional and important that you respond to the message and say so. Please *please* understand this, as too many people at all ages do not. If not, that task falls through the cracks and affects other people. It doesn't get more "real world" than that. If you tell us you are unable to get to something, another intern or team member can take care of it so a single beat is not missed. We'll discuss this in more detail in the following chapter, but take pride in what you are doing, no matter how boring it seems. Doing a database entry? Copy and paste the information so mistakes aren't made. As later on when a team member needs to grab that information, if it's wrong, it slows down work and progress for everyone. What seems boring and mindless has real effects on others, so please take it seriously.

I have to note here that although most folks aren't fans of email, I've had students admit that their attempts to bypass it have failed. Students will sometimes tell me they have their own communication systems that work quite well for them. I used to be totally open to this. Until I realized that perfectly motivated and hardworking students were missing tasks time and time again. We'd then sit down and go through their processes. The aforementioned Dan began his internship with his own systems, which ultimately broke down, and concluded the summer by saying: "I really don't see any other way of working within the industry other than with the email skills you taught me."

I have one young co-manager who would mention things about projects in relation to an artist during the beginning of our time working together. My other co-manager and I (there are 3 managers working with this artist) were out of the loop on many of these issues. We quickly realized that he had been Facebook chatting with colleagues in the industry as well as the artist. Although he had good intentions and there are of course countless ways to communicate, it's really important to set a precedent with colleagues and clients in a professional manner. In this instance, I insisted that the co-manager communicate internally via Slack and externally via email to ensure everyone was kept in the loop and high professional standards were met. Email is considered the global professional standard across industries; social media chat is not.

Don't get me wrong, we work in a social world and my experiences are drawn from a fun industry. Facebook chat all you want about concerts and music. Live shows are part of our industry, so oftentimes these conversations naturally blend into work. But make it clear, especially when working in teams, how the group is going to communicate so everyone stays informed and of course follow the standards of your particular internship and field.

Many internships will give you your own email address with your actual name on it. What an honor! There is responsibility that comes with this. It is **your** name on that email address, despite it being the company's domain. I have a natural aptitude for responding to all emails quickly and I do so generally within 24 business hours.

This means I have been building my network and reputation for reliability since day one of my internships. I strongly encourage you to do the same. If you are asked to do something via email and don't do it, of course it makes the company look bad. But ultimately the company is already established and most likely successful. You are not (yet). Take pride in your business communication, be enthusiastic, and build a strong reputation from day one.

At the same time, you never know how answering every message will help you in the future. I've had world class photographers contact me saying I gave them their first ever photo pass to a Dresden Dolls concert when they were in college. Because I responded to these people years ago and treated them with respect, they now want to help me. I see that a lot in the entertainment industry, but of course this is applicable to business in general.

The lesson? Don't be "above" anyone you're communicating with. Our entertainment firm takes pride in responding to everyone. You never know where that person will be someday, and frankly, it's just a polite thing to do! Not to mention that it's great business karma. It does not surprise me that when I reach out to folks, I almost always get a response. I'd like to think that writing back to people over the years has something to do with it.

EMAIL 101: HELPFUL HINTS FOR REAL-WORLD EMAILS THAT GET RESULTS (AND RESPONSES!)

Email is a very new concept for most students I encounter. Ultimately communicating via email is pretty limited in college. Then suddenly students are in an internship or graduate and literally don't know what to say in an email. Or they send emails that are too long or disorganized.

Here are the basics of modern business email:

- Subject line: Don't leave this blank. Describe the thread in as efficient and informative terms as possible. Not only does it look weird when one receives a blank subject email, the recipient will have no idea what it's about later when searching their inbox for information related to a specific project.

- Put spaces in before and after the body of the email, in between paragraphs, etc. This is super important as it looks professional and makes it easy to read for the recipient. At the same time, don't have too many paragraphs! Keep email messages short and to the point—it will increase the likelihood of the receiver responding and actually doing what you're asking of them.

- All fonts need to be the same in emails; there should be no different colors, shapes, or sizes. Crazy fonts are stressful to read on the receiving end. Why put the recipient in that position? You are most likely interning for a professional company and most folks do not want unprofessional looking emails. Many mail clients and webmail platforms have options to "make plain text" so all content is uniformed for the recipient and not all over the place. Utilize this option before sending to maximize email formatting and font efficiency.

- This is not required, but I am big on email clients. Apple Mail, Polymail, Airmail, Spark, Mail Pilot, Outlook, and Entourage are email clients that have been business standards for the past decade or so. This will help with formatting and organization to ensure you don't miss a single message. I've had many interns proclaim to be "Gmail whizzes," only to miss messages due to many of Gmail's default settings. Generally, once you work within an email client, you don't go back. Email and technology are of course constantly evolving. Check out Product Hunt to find the latest and greatest third party email apps.

- **Do not** send attachments over 5 MB. It is annoying to the recipient as it may clog or crash their Inbox. Dropbox and temporary file storage/link creation sites such as Hightail are your friends. We will discuss Dropbox in the following chapter. Most email clients will tell you how large the file is that you're attaching for easy reference. You can also CMD + I on a file on Macs or right click on PCs to find out a file's size.

- Keep emails short and to the point. If beyond a reasonable length, pick up the phone to communicate the message. Here are some basics with regard to salutations in email communication in most modern business environments:

- *Greeting.* Hi (first name),

- *Body of Email.* (Keep this short and sweet.)

- *Closing Salutation.* Thanks, Best, and Take Care, are just a few appropriate salutation examples. This helps humanize you to whomever you're emailing, in addition to being polite. It might seem unnecessary, but these details ensure the messages feel and look a lot better on the receiving end.
- *First Name*
- *Full Name*
- *Company Signature*

Ask your supervisor if they have a preference on email signature format. I generally go with:

Emily White
(O): +1 (This indicates it is my office phone number and the +1 is the U.S. country code since I have international colleagues.)
www.WhitesmithEnt.com

Some beg to differ, but I don't feel that listing one's email is necessary as the receiver has it from what you are sending them already.

REPLY, REPLY ALL, AND BCC

The following paragraphs are taken directly from my company's "Intern Manifesto":

We are aware you may not have been taught the importance of these three functions in school or even know what these functions mean. We are awesome at them and you will soon learn the ways of efficient emailing.

Be aware of when you are just replying to one person when you should have "replied all" to the group so everyone who needs the information on the chain receives it. At the same time, it's semi-annoying when the receiver has to copy people back in when one has replied instead of replied all to keep the group in the loop.

Similarly, be mindful of when you are unnecessarily replying all. Most people receive tons of emails all day and do not need any unnecessary messages. This is a nice courtesy for outside colleagues as well. With regard to clients, we often have to keep them focused, so an extra email may mean that important/relevant information is now buried.

If you want to provide information that the group needs, but also know that someone might reply "Thank you," address the recipients in the BCC field so busy team members aren't caught up in extra emails via these well-intentioned niceties. All of this helps us to continue to move work and our clients' careers forward by creating an efficient communication workspace. In short, moving the group to BCC when responding to something they don't need to be in the loop on moving forward shows that you have acknowledged the email but avoids dragging others into an unnecessary chain. It's common etiquette to state "Moving Jane and Bob to BCC" when doing so, therefore the receiver also knows that the group is in the loop about the response but doesn't need to be bogged down with future and unnecessary messages on a topic that might not be pertinent to them.

EMAIL FIELDS

- "To" in an email is pretty self-explanatory. If the company you are interning for has given you a company email address, update the settings on your devices to show your first and last name; this will ensure you are presented in a professional manner. While some email addresses will default this way automatically, you will need to set up others manually.

- "CC" stands for "carbon copy." This field is for looping in another team member who needs access to the information. For example, the rule at my entertainment firm is to "copy me always." And I really do read everything. That way I don't miss a single detail regarding what is going on with the company. I can also jump in to help if a team member strays a bit off track and offer assistance, guidance and experience to projects.

- The "BCC" field stands for "blind carbon copy." Use at your own risk! There are a few folks I trust to be aware when I BCC them, but one of the best things about email is it provides a written record. Therefore, if you BCC someone and they reply all, the folks who didn't know that person was actually copied now see that you BCC'd someone, making them wonder why you were hiding this fact.

  An important general rule is that **I don't put anything into email or digital form that I'm not ok having posted on the Internet.** (Ask Anthony Weiner if he wished he had followed this rule.) In the professional world, you might accidentally expose a piece of internal and/or confidential information when you BCC the wrong person. It's a great tool if you want to send yourself a copy of something or loop in a team member without inundating the recipient with what can seem like an overwhelming amount of folks. As with all business practices, use common sense with BCC. Think before you act, as your brain and intuition will more often than not lead you down the right path.

EMAILING OUTSIDE OF THE COMPANY

At our entertainment firm, I have a rule to not email anyone outside of our company's domain without asking. We will talk more about what is appropriate and inappropriate behavior with regard to pro-activeness in Chapter 8. But for now, I recommend asking your supervisors before you take it upon yourself to email outside of the company with the company's domain in your email address.

In my world, I've seen interns email other companies to ask for information about issues that our team already knew. It's really important that we save our communications with these companies for when we actually do need something. I've also seen clients emailed without permission. When this happens, sometimes the intern asks them for information we already have on file, which makes our company and team look unorganized, sloppy, and unprofessional.

Beyond that, our clients are *very* busy and creative folks. I often send them one email a day with all applicable information neatly organized and bullet pointed so they aren't distracted by countless messages from our team. That way they know to really focus in on the one message we send them and get back to us to keep their careers moving forward. Apply the same tactics to your world. Send people you're communicating with one email with minimal bullet points for each item, instead of three emails. You'll get more efficient responses this way and reduce other folks' stress. Yay!

CLEARING YOUR INBOX: YES YOU CAN!

Taken directly from our Intern Manifesto: *We expect you to clear your inbox every business day. This will help you stay on top of things and start fresh every day with a clear brain, tackling each project as it comes as opposed to constantly playing catchup.*

It only relatively recently came to my attention that this tactic has a name and it is "inbox zero." It sounds daunting, but is possible. By employing this tactic, I went from always feeling behind to fully being on top of my work. When you do get behind, don't be too hard on yourself.

It happens to all of us. One strategy to get through work is to turn your internet service off and reply to all emails offline via your mail client (note that Polymail does not support this as of this writing). That way you aren't distracted or inundated with messages while you are catching up, and aren't creating more mail for yourself by sending outward messages that you'll ultimately receive responses on while you are working.

Getting up super early works too. This is my own particular entrepreneur freak-ness, but sometimes I go to bed super early so I can rise at 4 AM. Doing work in the still of the morning ensures focus and minimal real-time responses. I've made it a pretty regular habit, but this strategy is also something to implement as you evolve and need to focus on a particular project for a set amount of time. That way you aren't waking this early every day, but only when you have a specific goal in mind.

SUNDAY NIGHT EMAIL PARTY

One tip I live pretty religiously by is clearing my inbox every Sunday night. Of course if you have something else going on, don't sweat it. But it's amazing the simple messages that come in over the weekend, and it's nice to prepare for the business week as well as set yourself up to start fresh with a clear-ish inbox Monday morning. I have former and present team members who swear that this tactic has changed their business lives for their own greater good.

A NOTE ON SMARTPHONES

Having a smartphone is pretty much essential in any form of modern business. I'm not saying that is right or healthy, but it is a reality. If you do not have a smartphone, communicate this to your supervisor. We would never require an intern to have a smartphone or work outside of office hours, but it's good information to know with regard to when we anticipate you seeing work communications; i.e., if there is a last minute guest list spot open for a concert we want to offer you. In this instance, we might think to text you to ensure you receive it instead of sending an evening email.

If you can't afford a smartphone, most folks totally understand that. If you can save up and obtain a used smartphone, build it the cheapest option on the market into your phone contract, or enter into a payment plan, it will be useful in helping you understand modern apps as you enter the business world. For example, did you know scanners are pretty much obsolete? We use scanning apps in addition to a plethora of other tools that have made modern business dealings easier and more efficient.

Those are some pretty solid email basics. As your career evolves, you'll continue to grow your voice and style over email as you gain experience. Also, don't fear Siri. Voice-based typing has been a godsend to my hands for a much needed break. But double-check any voice-based communications before sending, as the technology is not quite foolproof yet.

Now onto the phone!

PHONE 101: SKILLS TO MASTER ONCE YOU GET PAST THE FEAR

For whatever reason, many people fear using the phone. At one time I was one of them. I used to be scared to order a pizza when hanging with my friends in middle school (random and weird but true). Also, as mentioned, I was terrified when my initial task at my first ever internship was to call college radio stations. Now? I often have scheduled calls every hour on the hour during some days of the week. Phone skills are arguably more important at higher levels than email as you progress throughout your career trajectory. So keep this in mind to develop your phone skills sooner rather than later to help get ahead.

If you are asked to answer any sort of phones at your internship, please do it and with enthusiasm. I was thrilled and equally terrified when my internship supervisor at a major radio station asked me to cover the phones for her when she was on vacation. She was solely responsible for handling calls for the program director, who received *a lot* of important calls throughout the day. It was an honor to be asked and, with pride, I got through the week unscathed.

I also loved picking up the phone on incoming calls at the management company where I was trained. We had office managers for this, but as my best friend who was our office manager can attest, it was a great way to get to know folks in the industry. Not that you should be gabbing with them by any means, but said best friend (Laura) and I were able to humanize our phone answering exchanges at concerts and other events by saying to high level folks we met: "Don! I'm Laura from Madison House." They loved finally meeting the person whom they'd communicated with many times on the phone when calling for our bosses.

Before you jump in on covering phones, always ask about the etiquette of how the phones should be handled. If an intern at our company is asked to answer the phones quickly when someone is busy without time for explanation, here is a script we ask them to follow:

"Whitesmith Entertainment, this is (first name)."

(Presumably the person asks for someone at the company.)

"May I ask who is calling?" (This is where it *greatly benefits* you to know the name of clientele as well as folks in the industry. Mistakes will happen, but I've had clients upset if an intern answering the phone doesn't know who they are. This might seem egotistical, but it's true and I'm trying to save you from getting in trouble).

"They are out at the moment; may I take a message?" (Type whatever they say, even if it's just their name, in a Slack message or email).

"And what is the best number to reach you on?" (Take down the number if they give it to you. If it's a client, asking in this way isn't offensive as they may have a mobile and home line and will let you know where they are. If they just list the category and are a client who calls regularly, don't ask for the number. It looks unorganized if that information doesn't appear to be on file.

If you're able to get the company's preferences before handling the phone, ask if there is anything else you should know. I had a boss once who instructed us to tell everyone who called that he wasn't there. I didn't entirely understand that until I became the boss at my own firm. Most of the time I'm tied up in a project and it isn't efficient for me to stop the work flow unless the call is extremely important and/or time sensitive. That is why many folks (myself included) are big on scheduling calls.

Similarly, I ask that all call messages are emailed to me—even if I'm sitting there and it's literally my mom (no offense Mom!). We live in a world of such constant distraction that sending the email will ensure it doesn't slip my mind to call the person back. Though I usually remember to call Mom back, sending the reminder ensures she does get a call back! And this is also true of colleagues, of course.

THE PHONE IS YOUR FRIEND

From our company's Intern Manifesto: ***When a team member asks you to do something they should never have to follow up with you.*** This is absolutely the case for internal tasks. If your supervisor is asking you to do something twice, that is most likely not going to get you in their good graces. The same goes for external communications. If a supervisor has trusted you to obtain outside information, "I didn't hear back" isn't an acceptable answer. If that's the case, pick up the phone and call the person that you need information from, with permission to do so of course.

The average person is overwhelmed with e-messages. Even if you are keeping yours as efficient as possible, when that system fails, **call the person you are trying to reach**. Check with your supervisor first, but let them know you haven't heard back within a reasonable amount of time (two business days or so) and ask permission to call and follow up. Your supervisor will appreciate this so much more than if you say nothing and it becomes clear a week later that the task was never finished. The last thing you want is your supervisor following up with you about following up with someone else.

I promise you can get over your fear of the phone (if you have one like I did), and using it will become second nature. Developing a comfort level with the phone will ultimately be advantageous for you. Again, with permission, call people when you have not received a response via email.

Trust me, it works! Also, to be clear, *call* rather than text. We'll talk more about texting later in this chapter.

DIALING INTERNATIONALLY, SKYPE, AND GOOGLE VOICE

One of the biggest benefits of interning abroad is that dialing internationally has become second nature for me. I used to have to think hard about it, but this is no longer the case. Although you most likely will not need to do this until you are in an entry-level position, below is an overview on the basics for your reference:

The U.S. country code is +1. The + is now a symbol on most smartphones that can also be obtained by holding down "0" until "+" pops up. On landlines, it is generally dialed into the phone as 00 before the country code. Thus, if an international person was dialing a U.S. phone, it would be +1 area code or 001 area code, then the number.

Many folks are going to give you their regular in-country number, so this is often on you to figure out what their country code is. I'll use my UK mobile number as an example as it's turned off 99 percent of the time. So if you want to call it, have fun with that.

0790 6027 358 is how I would give that number to someone within the UK. For someone calling me internationally, the 0 is dropped and therefore the number should be +44 790 6027 358.

This is the case for many countries. So when in doubt, if there is a 0 listed initially and you are calling from outside of the country, drop the 0 after the country code and add +country code or 00 then country code before the non-zero numbers. If you're calling an international number while in that country, you can keep the 0 listed and more often than not, drop the country code. Oftentimes even smartphones will want you to dial out the entire number. So when in doubt, type in country code, no 0, and the remaining digits on the phone number.

It is expensive to make international calls from a landline and many mobile phones. Skype has been a business standard for years as it allows you to dial internationally for free. But, you have to have the other party's username to do so. A lesser known function of Skype is called "Skype

Out." Although you shouldn't be paying for anything, I'm teaching you this tool so you have it moving forward in your career. Skype Out allows you to call real phone numbers and not just usernames. I have a credit card associated with my Skype Out, and it bills me $10 a few times a year due to the international call rates being so cheap.

Incidentally, I have switched to T-Mobile for their incredibly reasonable international plans. Texting and data (a.k.a. email and the internet) is free internationally, as is calling folks over Wi-Fi. Free = even cheaper than Skype Out! Truly amazing.

I also want to mention Google Voice. This has been our office line for years. Google Voice allows me to point our office line to wherever I am in the world, which as I write this sentence, happens to be Thailand. Sometimes it points to my home line, or to my parents' line when I'm visiting them. I love this feature and encourage you to snag a Google Voice number for yourself.

That said, be aware that there can be some confusion associated with Google Voice. People text our number all of the time thinking it's my cell, even though signatures clearly state it's an office line. As minor as that is, it's worth mentioning as you always want to be mindful of others' communication preferences when possible. The point is always to get information across in a way that does not annoy the intended recipient. By keeping communications efficient, more will get done in a seamless manner.

A NOTE ON TEXTING

Texting is a casual form of communication, and it's important to know when to use it. In general in business, you should do so rarely and only when you need an answer urgently.

If you're communicating about a task externally, please email. If it's an internal matter and the company you intern for uses Slack, send your message that way. We start interns out on Level 1 type tasks, and although they are important and plug into the bigger picture, there are generally projects going on that take priority. If you have a question, please ask via Slack or email; supervisors don't need to be interrupted during their day to be asked where a file is. They'll get to it in due time.

If the company you're working at doesn't use Slack, don't send a second email on the same day to ask about your question again. It's not only going to bury your first message, but will most likely irritate your supervisor by continuing to overload their message box. It's not that they don't care about you or the task; it's that they might be super busy. So please do not add to this pile with a follow-up to your question on the same day.

I know you have the best intentions, but try to understand this from your supervisor's perspective. If 24 business hours have passed, feel free to ask them your question in person or, if you can, via Slack. Email a follow-up if you must (they may still be backed up), but avoid texting *unless it is crucial to get a real time response.* Use your judgment here. Running late to a meeting? Text the person to give them a heads-up, as they might be a sane and rational human who doesn't check email every second.

By the way, if you need to text someone internationally for any reason, WhatsApp will allow you to text internationally for free. (This is not preferred for interns, but I include it here as a good lesson for your general business knowledge.)

I recently discovered that a young brand rep who had just graduated college was texting one of my clients non-stop. I had no clue this was happening as industry standards are to go through management. It bothered the client and I had to ask the rep to communicate through me (which he should have been doing in the first place). This rep was incredibly well-intentioned, but again, blowing up someone's phone with texts is about as professional as Facebook messaging.

In short, strive to always project yourself as classy and high level in your communications. After all, you want to be treated and viewed with respect.

CONFERENCE CALLS & MEETINGS

If you are lucky enough to be asked to sit in on a company conference call or meeting, of course say yes! I try to involve interns in both so they get used to these important business settings.

If you are sitting in on a conference call, you need to understand it is not your place to participate (see Chapter 8 on "pro-activeness" when in doubt here, and/or ask your supervisor in advance of the call if need be). Also, please remember to mute your phone. That way you won't accidentally add unnecessary background noise to the call, which is both distracting for participants as well as embarrassing.

I was on a call once where a very intimidating boss had to tell an unknown person to stop breathing so loudly into the phone. And he was right! The breathing then immediately ceased. Mute is your friend! At the same time, of course don't forget to unmute yourself if you are in a position to speak (most likely once you are at your full time job, not as an intern).

Listening in on conference calls lets you build good instincts on knowing when to speak up, so people don't talk over each other. This is a skill that comes with time and practice. So listen, and be as thoughtful and efficient as possible. Also, be aware that while calls rarely go this long, it's a business standard in my world not to let them exceed an hour. Keep that hour time-budgeting in mind when planning your schedule now and for future use when you have more calls on your plate.

Also, as you evolve in your career, be sensitive that you don't waste the group's time. I'll generally call this out with a simple: "Please discuss this offline," if I see a logistical conversation between two team members starting to occur. While there is always an objective to a conference call, it's on all of us to be respectful of each other's time and to work as efficiently as possible.

This etiquette is similar for meetings. If you're lucky enough to be invited to sit in on a meeting, be polite and as old school as it sounds, speak when spoken to.

Whether sitting in on a call or meeting, offer in advance to take notes if no one is doing so and email them to your boss afterwards (or send to them in Slack if it's an internal meeting or call). This is a really useful thing you can do, as it will help participants retain information from the meeting.

MODERN OFFICE BASICS PART 1 WRAP-UP

Who knew there were so many business standards and etiquettes around the use of email and the phone? I'm thrilled you now have this guide to cut down on unnecessary and inefficient emails, as well as have learned tips on how to strengthen your phone skills. Now onto the ever-evolving Internet and even more basic skills you'll need to thrive in the modern workforce setting.

KEY TAKEAWAYS

Don't underestimate the importance of basic office tools and skills. How clearly and efficiently you are able to communicate with others—both inside and outside of your company—will directly determine your success as an intern. Learn, hone, and master these crucial "basics," including the modern communication etiquette tips detailed above.

Email skills are vital, especially for communicating with those outside your company. No one loves email but even with the rise of technology like Slack and Asana, it is here to stay. Learn to write succinct professional emails and respond to those you receive promptly and politely.

Read all email threads from the bottom up. You will be able to catch nuances that enable you to do the best possible job now and in future positions. You will also get to know "who's who" in your field and quickly pick up on industry lingo that will serve you well.

Make time to clean out your inbox. If need be, do it Sunday night or get up really early in the morning. This is time very well spent as it will keep you from falling behind during the workweek.

Overcome your fear of the phone. Almost everyone is intimidated by talking on the phone at first, but there is no better way to get answers out of people who are slow in responding to emails. You'll simultaneously make valuable inroads with others in your field by making human connections. Remember at the end of the day, the phone is your friend.

Resist the urge to text when you don't instantly get an answer to an email. Texting is a casual form of communication and should only be used when something needs to happen urgently. Be mindful of when to use which form of communication—email / Slack, text, and phone call in that order of category, is a good general rule based on the urgency of the information being conveyed.

Six

Modern Office Basics Part 2

From Google Drive to Dropbox & Social Media. +NOT Asking Questions That Are Google-able.

If you're in school, there are many modern tools in the workplace that you might have used only once in a while. A lot of these tools are also new to many staff members. That said, most of what is described here is pretty user-friendly, so it is likely that the folks you are interning for are quite well-versed in these platforms.

When I was coming up as an intern, it was the dawn of the digital era. I was often referred to as the company's "I.T. person." The irony is that, in reality, I would just Google solutions to whatever roadblocks came up, as well as play around with things until I figured out the answer.

At that time, it was expected that interns knew more about technology than their bosses. As mentioned, most of the people you intern for will use all of these tools on a regular basis and will expect that you know how to use them too. In the case that your supervisors are still getting the hang of these evolving technologies, it will benefit you significantly if you can help them to troubleshoot.

GOOGLE DRIVE: THE BACKBONE OF MANY BUSINESSES

Office standards have evolved from Microsoft Word and Excel into Google Drive (formerly "Google Docs"). Now, word processing documents, spreadsheets, and more are "shareable" items that can be viewed in real time. This is largely useful for team collaboration and reference, as opposed to trading attachments back and forth, which can easily cause confusion on data and information with different versions of documents floating around.

I'm currently writing this book in Google Drive. That way my literary agent, publisher, editor, and assistant can track changes as the project comes alive. I also don't have to fear writing a slew of text only to have it crash and disappear, as would happen from time to time in my college days on Word. Of course it's a pain when Wi-Fi goes out or is unavailable (though less so with T-Mobile's free tethering!). Yet, for the most part, Google Drive has allowed our team members to work from anywhere in the world in real time, never missing a beat.

At this time, you may want to be cognizant of what your Gmail account is or create one if you do not have one yet. Make sure it's professional— i.e., *not* something like 6969@Gmail.com—but don't think you can't have a fun with it. For example, I use my touring nickname as part of my personal Gmail address. Just keep in mind how you are presenting yourself.

Incidentally, I think Gmail is the most professional free domain you can use. Stay away from AOL email addresses, if you even know or remember what that is. Of course your school email address is fine, but you may not have access to it forever, so setting up a Gmail account tends to makes the most sense.

Once you have that rolling, start playing around in Google Drive. To create a document in the current version of Drive as of this writing, click on "Create" and then "Document." A very simple blank word processing page will appear. Play around with it. If you haven't done this already, write your next paper here as well as upload your résumé.

Note that you can download documents in various file formats, from Word to PDFs, and can access these items from wherever you are (assuming there is phone/internet service). Google Drive also has a fantastic app that I constantly use to access company information instantly when on the go. It also has various features to save information "offline" in case you are concerned about having access in low service/no Wi-Fi areas.

The same goes for spreadsheets in Google Drive. Click "Create" and then "Spreadsheet," and poke around with the various functions and features. I have discovered that most students do not know how to use formulas in spreadsheets. These are really helpful shortcuts and tricks to ensure the computer does math for you and you're not stuck doing it manually, which can lead to mistakes. Check out FiveMinuteLessons.com for reference on spreadsheet formula basics and other great office tips.

Keep your Google Drive organized from day one. Put things into folders with labeled categories that make sense. The labels can be as simple as school, personal, and work. This will help you to move forward and is a good habit to develop early on.

As you evolve into the business world, don't forget to ask colleagues and coworkers which email address they'd like Google Drive items shared with. In my world, all Google Drive elements live in my Gmail so everything is in one place. It's a pain when people share it with one of my company's domains, because I then have to log in and out and go back and forth between items. I'm not an old lady yet and already have more carpal tunnel syndrome than I'd like (and am grateful for Siri and voice-based technology!). It's amazing how all of those clicks and typing add up over the years, so be mindful on helping your bosses and team members cut down unnecessary clicks.

Our office also uses Google Drive spreadsheets for database storage and access. We start interns off at the most basic level in hopes that they master the task and think about how it plugs into the bigger picture. Although data entry might seem like the most unglamorous task ever, it is crucial that you get in the habit of copying and pasting information instead of typing it out.

I literally saw a professional reach out to an athlete today with an offer, only to have the athlete contact me saying he didn't receive the email. Upon further inspection, the professional had NOT copied and pasted the athlete's email address I had shared with him, resulting in the error and delivery delay of information. If I typed every piece of data or email address I ever had to communicate, I would surely make typos all the time. So get in the habit of copy and pasting email addresses and other data points, so that nothing is lost and time is not wasted.

> I frequently spot negative attitudes towards the task of data entry. For example, a student may think data entry is beneath them and may not copy and paste the information into our databases. When I go to grab that email address to make a pitch on a strategic day and time of the week (often Tuesdays midday), I may receive a bounce back message a few hours later. In that moment, I realize that an intern mistyped the information that I copied and pasted. Often times I am in a meeting and may not see the delivery error until the evening. Then suddenly it's Wednesday, and the week starts flying by, and the pitch may now have to go out the next week.

Everything you do as an intern has real effects, no matter how basic the task may seem. In the meantime, there is an open opportunity for you to grow beyond just doing what you are asked, which is the least of what your supervisor wants. Read the email that was sent to you from the bottom up with the contact information or data you are implementing. Google who that person is that you're putting into the company's database, and get to know names within your industry; follow them on Twitter if they pique your interest. I started my career knowing no one in the entertainment industry. Now I know countless people in the field. One by one, you are growing your network and knowledge of your industry with every database entry.

ALL ABOUT FILE FORMATS
As we segue into how to transfer files, I want to take a moment to discuss file formats. I have never seen this topic covered in a general academic setting. This is definitely an area that is assumed knowledge in business, but it can (understandably) be overwhelming and confusing. A master list

can be found at Wikipedia.org/wiki/List_of_file_formats, but that is only if you can't find what you need on the list below.

Don't feel like you need to know everything on the master list mentioned above. Instead, get fluent and confident with all of the below, as these are the most common file formats you will encounter at your internship and beyond:

- .DOC or .DOCX are Microsoft Word extensions for a document.
- .XLS and .XLSX are Microsoft Excel extensions, with CSV, ODS, and TSV almost always containing spreadsheets as well.
- .PPT: Microsoft PowerPoint extension.
- .PDF: Portable Document Format. In theory, a PDF cannot be edited, but a quick Google search pops up free tools to help you edit PDFs if need be (we have used PDFescape for years).

I want to pause for a moment and point out that one can download all of the above file formats via Google Drive. Simply click "File," select "Download as," and choose your file format of choice. .DOC is a safe bet for documents someone may need to edit, as is XLS for spreadsheets. Go with PDF if the plan is not to have the document edited further; it will be slightly cleaner, easier, and less cumbersome to open in PDF format on the receiving end than a Microsoft document.

- .JPEG, .TIFF, and .GIF are all generally images. When in doubt, go with JPEG.

IMPORTANT NOTE: Even if a PDF looks like an image, it is not an image. You cannot upload it to Facebook, Twitter, and other social media. Although looks can be deceiving, a PDF is a document, NOT a photo. Send photos as JPEGs to help streamline workflow. And as you have learned, be mindful if emailing attachments to keep it under 5 MB. You'll learn how to create a link to transfer larger files via Dropbox in the next section.

- .MP3 and .WAV are individual music files. MP3s are the most common and they vary in quality (the higher the MB / larger the size of the file, the higher the quality), while WAVs are very high quality (and therefore larger) music files.
- .PNG is a screenshot image (Command, Shift, 3 on Macs; PrtScn on PCs).
- .PSD is a Photoshop file.
- .TXT is a general text file. This does not always open for some folks, so stick with PDFs and Word documents as mentioned above.
- .ZIP is an extremely common extension for compressed files, which we'll explain in the next section on Dropbox and file sharing. Again, be mindful of ZIP file sizes if emailing as an attachment. If over 5 MB, keep reading to learn all about Dropbox.

DROPBOX, DATA, CALENDARS, AND YOU: A QUICK PRIMER

Dropbox is a common cloud-based storage tool that is used across industries, though Amazon, Google, and others also offer these services.

The music and entertainment industries are content-based fields. My company has an asset management system within Dropbox in which we store key materials for our clients as well as for easy reference internally.

I encourage you to set up a Dropbox account; it's free to get started. As mentioned, do not ever send an email that contains over 10 MB of data. I know we said 5 MB before, but 10 MB is really the limit to not irritate people or mess with their inboxes. If data sizes confuse you (as they did me for years), learn! <u>And if there is ever anything you have a question on, **Google it**. (More on this shortly!)</u>

If you have photos, music, or content to send for work or personal reasons, save it in a folder on your desktop and control click (Mac) or right click on the folder to "compress" or "zip" the folder. Then upload the zipped folder to Dropbox and a link will be created in which you and others can then easily download the contents without clogging inboxes along the way.

Similar to Google Drive, get in the habit of keeping your Dropbox organized. And if you see things out of order in company Google Drive and Dropbox platforms, ask if you can help clean it up. That used to be an internship standard in the physical world. If you saw a mess (say, a pile of unorganized CDs in a music office), you were considered a good intern if you organized it without being asked. This showed that the intern was thoughtful and aware. Of course that's not what you go to school for, but it's a nice and polite gesture that people will really appreciate whether you're an employee or an intern.

On all shared company documents, follow previous formatting with regard to fonts, sizes, and formatting. Interns are supposed to help keep things in order, not make them disorganized. If you see mistakes or outdated information, ask if you can make updates to keep the documents aligned. Take pride in helping to keep work organized, as it helps others and will benefit you as this is a great skill that can become second nature over time. These details help teams and companies to stay focused and on task, which ultimately is the foundation of businesses.

I've tried to keep the information in this book relatively general so it is applicable to multiple fields. That said, play around with uploading (appropriate) content to YouTube and Instagram, work on hashtags, and other elements of metadata that your supervisors may expect you to know about. Similarly, if you are in music, please do the same in SoundCloud.

We use SoundCloud frequently to upload music privately for industry/internal use. We do the same in Dropbox, but that is generally for content we're okay with people downloading. SoundCloud has a great private streaming platform and also has a download option. Practice on these so if a boss asks you to upload content privately to SoundCloud, you don't leak someone's new material to the world by accident. A task this important should probably not be delegated to interns, but many supervisors wrongly assume that students have these skills. Precisely why I have written this book.

If you're uploading or posting anything publicly on behalf of the company, please check your work! I was horrified when an outgoing assistant uploaded an artist's new album to Bandcamp with the song titles misspelled. Take pride in your work, and know that what you do really affects others.

The same goes for any sort of calendar entries. No matter who or what you're entering information into a calendar for (most companies use Google Calendars as they are shareable), read the information back to yourself to ensure it makes sense. Put yourself in the reader's shoes. Do they know when, what, and where the scheduled item is? Is there a mobile phone number listed if it's an in-person meeting, or the office line noted if it's a call? Use full names (I have 19 people named Josh in my cell phone alone) and reference the company, as well as potentially what the meeting or call is about. These are critical details for busy folks and clients. At the same time, do not list any additional and unnecessary info into calendars unless specifically asked. Keep it clutter free, streamlined and organized for maximum efficiency. Everyone makes mistakes, but they should be minimal in the calendar and scheduling department whether you are CEO or on the first day of your internship.

If the wrong information is entered and it is an interview or flight, we might cause an artist to look like a diva by not showing up, or worse yet, literally miss the flight to where they have to go. We pay assistants to help with calendar entries as this information has to be as perfect as humanly possible. Also, be mindful to not creating extra entries. If there is a flight connection, put that in as one entry, not two. I have a lot of things in my calendar, as do other busy folks. So there is no need for two entries regarding the same item.

Be aware of **time zones** as many businesses work in the global marketplace. This is also especially relevant for travel. I have my calendar entries written out for the times regarding where I am in the world. Get to know EST, PST, GMT, and other time zones relevant to your internship and field's markets, and always double-check time zone differences (Google for this information!). Remember to take into account daylight savings, as this alters the time difference. Remember that not all countries' daylight saving falls on the same day as the U.S., if indeed they observe it at all.

Here are some formatting examples for you to reference:

Example: Meetings
10:30 AM EST: Meet w/ Jessica Weitz & Barry from MCT Management for a general catch-up: Address; Phone number.

Example: Calls
2 PM EST: Call Brooke Parrott from Songkick about artist promotions: Phone number; Brooke is calling Emily.

Example: Flights
11:45 AM CST: FLIGHT: BNA to LGA via AA #4653 arriving @ 2:50 PM; Confirmation: CKLNOY

SCANNING AND E-SIGNATURES

As mentioned, scanners are now obsolete for the most part via scanning apps available on smartphones. If you do not have a smartphone, ask how your company prefers you handle scanning.

Similarly, keep in mind there are apps that make signing documents quick and easy, saving the pain and trees involved in physical printing. Sites like HelloSign.com and SignNow.com, for example, allow you to sign documents online without having to print and scan.

SHIPPING 101: USPS, FEDEX, UPS & SHYP

Mailing things used to be an intern standard. With the decline of physical documents, this skill has gone out the window. Some feel that I shouldn't include this section of the book. At the time of this writing, the last time I asked an intern to FedEx something, they were totally overwhelmed as they had never done that before. (I want to interject here that most likely you haven't yet done many of the things you will do at your internship.

We'll talk about this later on, but definitely try to Google it or otherwise figure it out before you ask—you'll most likely figure it out and learn problem-solving skills along the way.) I asked the aforementioned intern if I should include a how-to guide on shipping in this book, and they said, "Yes please!"

For this section, I'm going to turn it over to my best friend Laura Keating, who is a world-class merchandise person for bands, product manager for artists and labels, as well as the former office manager at my first job out of college. She is the physical world shipping queen! Laura writes:

> In the online era of instant information delivery, sending a physical object to a different location may seem overwhelming with the myriad of options and restrictions. But shipping anything, from an urgent document to a giant sculpture, can be extremely simple if you just know where to look.
>
> The **United States Postal Service (USPS)** is still the most convenient and least expensive option for shipping anything around the world from the U.S. There is a post office in every town across America, and while the lines can be long, its process of shipping is simple. Depending on what you're shipping and how quickly you'd like it to arrive at its destination, there's a large selection of pricing options and they are all laid out very clearly on USPS.com.
>
> The post office provides free shipping materials for Priority Flat Rate that removes the headache of searching through your building's recycling to find the perfect box. And thanks to a variety of online shipping apps (i.e., Stamps.com), you can order free shipping supplies to be delivered to your home, process and pay for the shipment, print a label, and leave your package by the mailbox for your local mail carrier to collect. <u>You never have to leave your home or office</u>.
>
> Please be aware that USPS has a major downside—delivery times are not guaranteed and can often be delayed for no

apparent reason. So check with your supervisor to ensure you are mailing your task via their preferred method.

United Parcel Service (UPS), **FedEx** (short for **Federal Express**), and **DHL** are the major privatized shipping companies. They have similar rates and services, and are best used for shipping items that must arrive at a specific location at a very specific time. They guarantee delivery within the number of days you paid for (2 day, 3 day, or overnight). Sometimes weather or disasters can delay these times (also known as "acts of God"), but for the most part UPS, FedEx, and DHL stick to their schedules.

UPS/FedEx/DHL downsides: They are more expensive and you may have to drop the package off at a UPS or FedEx store, as scheduling a pickup is an additional fee, and you have to be home to sign for the pickup. Also be aware that sometimes these services won't deliver to very remote locations. Again, check with your supervisor as most companies have accounts with one or all of these carriers, which also helps the company save money on shipping costs.

As a touring merchandiser, it's one of my responsibilities to make sure merchandise arrives at each show on time with the band paying the least amount of money to get it there. I've had a few major shipping catastrophes over the years trying to get boxes of t-shirts delivered on time before the band is off to a different city. Again, thanks to the miracle of the Internet and specifically social media, I've discovered that crowdsourcing your shipping is sometimes the best and only option. This tip is more specific to touring. If a venue confirms they will not be open to receive a package, we have often sent merchandise to trusted friends or fans, who receive free merchandise from us and tickets to the show as a thank-you! Ultimately, plan ahead and be aware of local/international "bank" holidays; something Emily and I had to learn the hard way as young touring crew members abroad years ago.

Here is an example of a scenario in which I got creative and did whatever it took to get the goods to where they needed to be in time for a show. I needed to have merchandise to a concert venue in Houston before 6 PM on a Thursday, but online tracking was showing that the last scan for the packages was at the sorting facility 20 miles from downtown, and doors to the venue were opening before they said it could be delivered (which meant fans would be in the venue wanting the merch before it was there). Calls to UPS just came back with the same answer.

Due to weather delays, the boxes had never made it out of the facility and onto the delivery truck, yet the boxes were scheduled to be delivered the following day. Well, by the following day, my artist would be hundreds of miles away in Dallas, and we would have missed our chance to sell merchandise at the Houston event. The artist let me use her Twitter account to ask local fans who might live or work close to the sorting facility to go pick them up in exchange for free tickets to the sold-out show. We ended up with the merchandise at the show on time, and a lovely fan got to see the concert for free. This is a great reminder to get creative when solving a problem if the traditional road has a block to get you to the end goal of the completed tasks.

In all instances, be aware of whether or not your boss wants insurance on what you are shipping. Similarly, you may have to fill out customs forms if the package is going internationally, so be prepared for this. At the same time, don't be intimidated! Customs forms ask for basic information that you can fill out one field at a time.

Beyond major shipping companies, there are also local couriers in cities like New York that will get items across town within the day. More likely, it makes sense for YOU to be the courier, which is also a great way to get to know your way around the city or area of your internship. But we have had interns order couriers before, and they will come to you. This is generally a rather pricey option, so as always, please follow all instructions from your supervisor.

And finally (especially for the burgeoning touring crew member!) there are freight services. If you need to ship a piece of gear, furniture, a car, or a 25 foot tall metal sculpture, there are lots of freighting companies that will come to you to collect whatever it is you need to move. You will most likely not be in charge of shipping such a large item at your internship, but you never know! Similar to a courier, use the one closest to you that is well rated and offers the best rates if your boss does not have a preference. In the music world, we generally work with specialized touring freight companies, such as Sound Moves and Rock-It Cargo.

When in doubt and if in a major city, check out Shyp. It's a great app I've been using when I don't have time to explain all of the above to interns. For $5, someone will turn up and deal with shipping for me. Hooray!

Additionally, although this isn't the case for all companies of course, I wanted to mention that if I put something on an intern's desk, it usually means we need something done with it. I generally remember to message the intern what it is and what to do, but if something appears on your desk, ask what it's about. Maybe it was left there by accident, or maybe it's something for you to do. Don't let it slip through the cracks if it's the latter.

POSTS, TWEETS AND HASHTAGS: THE BASICS OF SOCIAL MEDIA

Many internships will assume that you have basic knowledge of social media posting and marketing. I've seen students note this as a skill on their résumé, and then they turn up and don't actually know how to create a proper social media post. Having your own personal social media accounts alone doesn't necessarily count as having skills in this department.

For in-depth social media marketing skills, check out Ariel Hyatt's books. In the meantime, here are some tips if your boss asks you to post something on the company's or a client's social media accounts:

- Time of day is crucial for posting effectiveness. I generally recommend 1 PM EST for U.S. based companies so you hit the West and East coasts, as well as Europe, Africa, and South America, when people are up and online (no offense Asia and Australia!). Facebook allows you to schedule posts if you aren't available during that time, and apps like Hootsuite do the same for Twitter and Instagram. Same for the day of the week. Defer to your supervisor, but Tuesday/Wednesdays are generally the most effective versus weekends, Fridays, Mondays, or holidays.

- Please, please, please put a period (.) in front of @ if beginning a post with a Twitter handle. Otherwise, only followers of both the account you're tweeting from and the person who is mentioned will see it; thereby greatly diminishing your results. Beginning a Twitter post with an @, communicates to the platform that it's a conversation between two users; not an original post for all followers. I have to say this over and over to interns, but you get to learn it here (ideally) before your internship! Similarly, you *don't* need a period in front of an @ if there is a non-tagged word in front of it. Play around with your own Twitter feed to get the hang of all of this until it becomes second nature. As we will discuss in Chapter 9, your social media accounts are a way to build and maintain your professional brand and online network as well. So you want it to look right and not be sloppy.

- Be aware of the company's "voice" and style. You may have picked this up already from your pre-internship research as you have (hopefully) been following the company's social media accounts before you even began your internship. If you are asked to draft a post for the company's social media, when in doubt, run the draft by your supervisor and/or the person who asked you to do this task to start to learn exactly what they want to go in posts. They'll most likely give you the information, but just in case, this is an area to double-check copy with your supervisor as the words you post will go out to the entire world immediately. Don't be intimidated by that! Take a deep breath, as well as a meditation break if you need it, to get focused and start to learn this crucial skill.

- Tag, hashtag, and tag some more! To engage with and ensure that the maximum amount of people possible see your post, tag any and everything in your post as well as add relevant hashtags. In my world, if we're announcing a concert, we tag the venue, the other artists on the bill, and hashtag the city. If posting a piece of press, tag the outlet and journalist as they'll most likely re-tweet it or push it out further to their followers, making it an inherently viral post by nature (albeit in a small, but effective way). Hashtags are particularly effective on Instagram.

- Know that Facebook is very ad-heavy and as a platform, is going to favor posts that are paid advertising campaigns, even if it's a small amount. If someone asks or questions why Facebook posts aren't getting as many likes/comments/views as one wants or as in past years, know that is why. At the same time, I encourage those who want more people to see their Facebook posts to do a low ad spend. You don't need to spend $100/day to get results; work within your budget here (this is more of an FYI for general business, not necessarily specific to interns).

- Use goo.gl or Bitly for shortened links to post efficiently with clean formatting on Facebook. Twitter will shorten links automatically.

As you can see, social media posting is a real skill. Many companies take it for granted and think it's simple, and expect anyone younger than them to know what they're doing. Prove that you do have base social media skills with all of the above and maybe the company will create a position in digital marketing just for you. You never know until you try!

PRIVACY = PROFESSIONAL

My companies have all interns and team members sign non-disclosure agreements (NDA). This is to not only protect company and client information from getting out, but also to remind all team members to not have big mouths if they're out with friends so they'll hopefully think twice about mentioning something that our clients might not want the world to know. **If your internship does not have you sign an NDA, pretend that you did.**

You don't want to lose your internship or create a reputation for yourself of not being trustworthy. In short, if you yap about confidential and private company information, you'll come off as immature and unprofessional. People may not tell you what is confidential information and what isn't. So when in doubt, keep information to yourself. And as always, use common sense, your best judgment, and basic manners at all times; whether you're at your actual internship or attending social work functions. As a general rule, if the information is public, spread it far and wide! If not? Keep it to yourself.

BE A PROBLEM SOLVER: DON'T ASK QUESTIONS THAT ARE "GOOGLE-ABLE"

From our company's Intern Manifesto: *We have noticed that many students do not try to solve a problem before asking someone for a solution. Oftentimes when a student does try to figure out the task at hand, they not only solve the problem, they also save their supervisor time. This allows everyone to continue to move forward for the greater good of our clients and projects, but the student/intern has also learned an important skill when this happens: the ability to problem solve. This will help you with your careers and lives in general.*

If there is anything you take away from this book to help you in your career, it is this. So highlight, rip this page out, post it on your desktop; do whatever you need to do. Generally speaking, you will get farther in life by trying to figure things out yourself, before asking. DO NOT confuse this with the oft misguided advice to "be proactive." We are talking about problem solving basic intern tasks that you are given; not taking what could be unnecessary, but well-intended, "initiative." We'll talk more about how to handle the urges of wanting to be "proactive" in Chapter 8.

To that point, when you try and figure things out before asking, a team member should never be presented with a question in which the answer is **"Google-able."** This is a frustrating waste of time. It also does not make you look good to verbally ask someone for information that Google can answer for you or that your supervisor will then need to Google search for. So think before you ask, and try to avoid interrupting your supervisor's workflow.

I've had students ask me what the office's address is, prompting me to wonder how they got there in the first place that day. Similarly, I've heard colleagues express frustration when interns with smartphones ask them how to get somewhere. Google's Maps app is your friend and will generally know the best route by public transportation, foot, car, or bike.

In short, this is **your** internship. Take pride in your tasks and what you are doing. Your colleagues and the team around you will notice. If you begin your career with this mentality and take it through every job you ever encounter, it will ensure a long and robust professional experience.

KEY TAKEAWAYS

Learn Google Drive and Dropbox inside and out. These tools are quickly becoming business world standards. Keep both of these accounts organized and build good habits starting now. Incidentally, your company will appreciate you taking the initiative to organize their Dropbox account (ask them first of course). Believe it or not, it's simple extra tasks like this that will make you shine as an intern.

When doing data entry (inside Google Drive or elsewhere), copy and paste whenever possible. When you key in information, it's too easy to make a mistake that can really screw up someone's workday. TAKEAWAY

WITHIN A TAKEAWAY: Everything you do as an intern has real world effects and they can be devastating. Be mindful. Be careful.

Be aware that shipping still matters. Yes, the digital era has made the mailroom far less central to the intern experience than it once was. But things still need to be shipped, and you still need to know how to do it. Learn the pros and cons of different shipping methods so you'll know which to use when. And of course always ask your supervisor on preferences before proceeding.

Know the basics of social media. No, having your own Instagram and Twitter doesn't count. Read up on this subject as you may well be asked to post something. Fair or not, many old school business people assume you are social media savvy due to your age. Don't disappoint them.

Google first. Ask questions later. Asking a question that can easily be answered with a few simple key strokes only frustrates your supervisor and interrupts their work flow. Don't do it! The ability to problem solve is so important—not just in your internship but in your larger career and life.

Seven

Making Yourself
Indispensable

The Key to Success. +What to Do When There is "Nothing" to-do.

A career-changing piece of advice I remember being given in college over and over seemed both simple and daunting at the same time: make yourself indispensable.

The idea was to become a part of the workforce culture as an intern, so much so that the company can't imagine not having you around. I began seeing a shift in this concept a few years into running my company. Students weren't being given this advice. Instead they were told that if they interned, that would qualify them to land a job based on that internship existing on their résumé. Better yet, one's internship could even lead to getting hired at the company one is interning at.

As we've discussed, it's not necessarily sustainable for a company of any size to hire every great intern that comes along. With the fierce competition that exists in sought-after industries, it's important to remember that you are building your skill set and network. That intertwined with hard work and a genuine spirit will lead to a career.

All of that aside, once you have your eyes set on a job (though I do encourage you to expand your horizons to a job category within your desired field versus a specific job, especially in the early stages of your career,) or are going after the field you want; the way to get there is to **make yourself indispensable**.

GETTING GOOD AT THE "GRUNT WORK": A.K.A. THE FOUNDATION OF EVERYTHING

So what does being indispensable mean exactly? My initial plan was to camp outside Marcus Russell's office (Oasis' manager and founder of Ignition Management), until they would let me in and do whatever it took to help them out in any capacity. My intention and path led me elsewhere and I couldn't be happier, but this spirit of tenacity really is the key to success: Be willing to do whatever it takes (within ethical reason of course) to enter the field of your dreams.

On a side note, it's great when Oasis' Noel Gallagher comes to town and I get to just be a fan. Meanwhile, my professional experiences led to Noel dedicating "Don't Look Back in Anger" to me at a festival in Europe when I was a young tour manager. Stay the course, work hard, and your goals and dreams may arise in ways you never expected.

But back to the work. For me, the philosophy of making myself indispensable became most apparent when I introduced myself to the singer of The Dresden Dolls, Amanda Palmer, when they played at my school. Further, when I wrapped up my first internship at Powderfinger Promotions, I was asked to stay, upon being told I was "one of the best interns" they'd ever had. **This was solely because I did what I was asked to do while also being polite, friendly, and saying yes to everything I was invited to. <u>That is the basis of making one indispensable.</u>**

> *Becoming indispensable is achieved by completing everything that is asked of you, doing your tasks well, working hard, attending as many events as possible, responding to all messages, being genuinely kind and professional, and staying on top of things as much as possible, while also learning and evolving in multiple ways.*

Ultimately, I didn't stay at Powderfinger and instead ended up making myself indispensable to The Dresden Dolls. It was rather perfect timing as a band on the verge of breaking has *a lot* going on and a lot to do, from grunt work to glamour; though, remember that the "glamour" is a very small percentage of working in entertainment.

INDISPENSABLE PRINCIPAL 1: ASK HOW YOU CAN HELP, THEN GET TO WORK HELPING.

When I asked The Dolls' frontwoman to let me know if she ever needed help with anything, I meant it. Of course I loved music, and dreamed of touring and working in the music industry. But I had no vision or expectation of what my offer to help would actually entail.

In reality, what Amanda Palmer needed help with most was typing emails. Hundreds of them. She had been running the band without a traditional team that would normally take care of everything from booking the band to public relations. Meanwhile, due to her aggressive keyboard playing style, Amanda suffered from tendinitis from the mix of performing as well as answering the countless emails surrounding the band.

I quickly took over all email duty. This typing work ranged from contacting industry folks, to fans, to personal e-blasts that the audience still adores. It was a lot. And although hanging out at a burgeoning rock star's house sounds like fun, ultimately it was work. Grunt work, busy work, physical work—you name it, I did it. With joy! It was my pleasure to help this great band and be a part of something so special and creative.

It really *was* fun to hang out at a rock star's house. Amanda lived in an arts collective that also housed filmmaker Michael Pope, The Dresden Dolls' web designers Thom and Steve Martin, amazing visual artist Zea Barker, amongst many others. It was only a few blocks from campus, but felt like being in Oz and was a break from my life as a college athlete, which was a specific world in and of itself. Those experiences were both influential and a blast. But it didn't change the fact that my first major task for the band was to take dictation from Amanda to help her get through the few hundred emails that came across her desk every day.

Most people do not enter the arts with a dream of typing emails. That said, this task gave me a significant amount of experience and insight. As what a wonderful way to get into my boss' head and understand the inner workings of a company (in this case, the "company" was a band).

INDISPENSABLE PRINCIPAL 2: GET USED TO FEELING INTIMIDATED (AND PUSHING PAST IT!)

Rather quickly, all of the artists in the building got used to having this broad-shouldered college swimmer (me) around to help Amanda and drummer / multi-instrumentalist Brian Viglione. The work also involved helping out in every way possible at local live shows. I was intimidated at first as I had limited technical knowledge of live sound or gear. So I did as I was asked and made my merch table look as gorgeous and inviting as possible. Within a few years, I had learned so much that I was as comfortable on a stage in between acts or shows as I was in my own home. In fact, one reason I decided to retire from tour managing at age 23, was that the venues were starting to feel more like home than my actual apartment.

The point is, I did what was asked of me not only without complaint, but I embraced it and did everything that was asked of me *as well as I possibly could*. While I did my tasks and focused on the things I did know how to do, every day I became more comfortable with my surroundings. These settings ranged from helping at the literal art house I was interning out of, to learning what to do with the cables strewn over a rock stage, to interacting with the people who worked at venues as well as band members and fans.

All of this was quite intimidating at first. But with dedicated work, focus, attention, and zero complaints, these surroundings and people eventually became as natural to me as the comforts of a work family.

INDISPENSABLE PRINCIPAL 3: BECOME A PROBLEM-SOLVING WIZARD.

Let's talk for a moment about this concept of doing tasks to the best of your ability—and what that means. Instead of constantly asking your supervisor for answers, use the Internet to solve problems and figure things out. You'd be amazed how many things are demonstrated even in a visual manner by searching on YouTube. Ultimately, tackling projects and problems this way is going to change how you think, and therefore change your life.

I often had bosses that were so busy and caught up in their own world that it would be *unthinkable* for me to constantly be asking questions. And this was when I was an employee, not even an intern. Instead, they would give me tasks, and I'd be told to "figure it out." I'm so glad I did. The problem-solving skills I developed due to not having my hand held is something I cherish every day. It has trained my mind to think about work differently, effectively solve tasks, and move forward across the board, day in and day out.

Of course, when you truly cannot figure something out after going through all of the above, ask your supervisor. This rule applies to everyone! One of my business partners specializes in comedy, film, and television. So when a question comes up in that world, I rely on her experience and expertise for accurate insight. It doesn't mean I can't generally figure it out myself, but having colleagues and mentors who know other things and/or more than you is obviously an asset beyond belief. At the same time, this partner is busy, so I can't constantly bog her down with every issue that comes up. I have to <u>save that interaction for when it's information I truly cannot obtain for myself, either by figuring it out or via internet-based research</u>.

Let's talk about internet-based research for a moment. The information you're looking for is there. Keep searching. Keep clicking. Don't leave any stone unturned. When I ask an intern to research an email address for me and they come up empty-handed, that is not a good thing.

Check LinkedIn, Facebook artist pages (in my world), Twitter links, and official sites. Try different combinations of Google searches to see what comes up in forums and other conversations deeply embedded into web-sites. Keep going; the information is there. And if it really isn't? Research how email addresses are set up at the company the person works at. If it's as simple as First.Last@Domain.com, you can at least let your boss know that this is your best educated guess for the contact information (though make sure to let them know it's an educated guess).

Also, as we've discussed, don't fear using the phone for your research purposes. Ask before calling another company, but if you're truly stuck or you're trying to figure out the name of the point person you're research-ing (i.e., if I need the email address of a particular artist's manager or agent, and we only have the company information), ask if you can give a call to investigate further. If granted permission, identify where you are calling from and ask if it is possible to learn the name of the agent you're seeking.

INDISPENSABLE PRINCIPAL 4: DON'T GET BORED; GET ON BOARD (WITH A GOOD ATTITUDE AND WORK ETHIC).

What if you are plagued with what seems like a completely different problem? Your tasks are too easy (or boring, mindless, or degrading). There is an idea that interning tends to be about getting coffee and/or mailing things. Considering we had to have a section in the book on how to mail things, clearly it's a skill that needs to be learned. And coffee? I feel you! I remember being offended when my boss at VH1 Classic asked me to get coffee for him and the other producers on an early morning shoot. Now, I realize how much stress and pressure he was under to film the piece they needed to air the following day with a small budget and limited time, as well as only so much daylight at a public location. He didn't have time to get coffee, and I was there to help in any way possible.

Let's bring it back to the office, and the menial or boring tasks you may be asked to complete. As mentioned, it is *very* rare that I would ever ask an intern to order lunch or pick up a caffeinated bever-age. In fact, I used to joke that I only drank strong caffeine (sugar-free

Red Bull was my beverage of choice as a tour manager) during "work emergencies."

If someone asks you to do such a thing, in the least, it's a helpful and nice thing for you to do. I encourage you to do so with a good attitude, instead of a negative outlook. *Pay attention* to what is going on around you! Is the office busy? Are people rushing about frantically? If I have to ask someone to handle a food or beverage order, it means I literally do not have 5 minutes to look at a menu and place an order, even in the age of on-demand delivery. It means that work is pouring out of every possible place and potentially a real work emergency is happening.

So listen up. Soak it all in. Observe everything you can. Do what is requested of you to the best of your ability beyond the food ordering. Know that assisting a very stressed-out boss is actually incredibly helpful, and more often than not your selfless act of helpfulness will be remembered. Most likely you'll be offered lunch or coffee for yourself as well (say yes and thank you). And even if you don't get acknowledgment or kudos, don't sweat it. <u>Remember that consistent work will get you ahead, not every specific piece of work you do</u>. Oftentimes, the work that you think will lead to something doesn't. Rather, it's the seemingly arbitrary tasks and experiences that put us on our path.

At the same time, I've read and seen interns gripe when someone is upset with them if a coffee or food order isn't right. Maybe it's the restaurant's fault or maybe you just made an innocent mistake. At any rate, no one will fire you for this. But one reason we start interns off with basic tasks is because we need to see that they can be trusted with responsibilities before moving them up the ladder to higher level tasks.

Am I going to freak out if there is regular milk in coffee instead of non-dairy? Or meat on a salad that I didn't ask for? No. But there are many people who will. And if those details aren't paid attention to, it may show your supervisor that they can't trust you to help on-site with clients who may be vegan, may have allergies, or won't stand for mistakes.

By taking pride in all tasks that you do, it shows your supervisor that you can be trusted with details. Details are generally the foundation of many businesses, so show that you can be trusted with a detail-oriented task, no matter how menial. This also shows that you can handle higher level detail-oriented tasks. If these mistakes on menial tasks continue to happen, it shows your supervisor that you do not have pride in what you are doing, and you could come off as being above helping. Don't be above anything; we're all here to help each other out, and again, by having a positive attitude and getting it right, it shows that you can be trusted with details, no matter what the task.

INDISPENSABLE PRINCIPAL 5: EMBRACE THE NITTY-GRITTY (IT PAYS OFF!)

I have one colleague that is now the president of a very successful music company. He got his start as an intern making copies at a major label. Boring right? Not if you're smart like he was and *read* the contracts of the superstar pop artists he was tasked with copying. Even if the task seems humdrum, there is always something to learn and knowledge to glean.

Everything that happens in a company is part of the entire structure, and it's important to not only think about all possible aspects of the task you are given, but also think about how it plugs into the bigger picture of the company. You'll learn new skills that lead to more knowledge for your career every step of the way.

For example, getting paid at the end of a concert is called "settling." If an artist sells enough tickets, there is "backend" money. Even at the shows where I knew the finances didn't break even and there were no extra funds for the band, I would go through every single number until I understood what it was for and why it was there to see if it matched the original agreement between the agent and promoter. This went from me looking at contracts when I was 19 that may as well have been written in another language, to becoming a whiz at settling within just a few years, always getting what my artists were owed, if not more. This was also in no small part due to my tour managing mentors Mike Luba, Chewy Smith, and Brendon Downey. Again, soak up every piece of knowledge you can get, whether direct or indirect. It's all around you.

THE RIGHT WAY TO BUILD WORK RELATIONSHIPS AND MAKE INROADS FOR YOUR CAREER

Say you've completed your tasks as you've been told. Now what? Every ambitious intern wants to continue to help. It's really important to be mindful and aware of what is going on around you. If your supervisor and/ or bosses seem engrossed in a project, don't interrupt them. If they have a headset on, know that they might be on the phone!

I felt bad for a young intern at my first job out of college when I saw him go up to a partner at the company for a casual chat. Not only was the boss on the phone via his Bluetooth headset, but he didn't have time even if he wasn't. I pulled the intern aside to ask what he was thinking and the response was that he was trying to "network." I explained that our boss was *very* busy and that there was a place and time for that. For example, he could come to one of our shows and talk to the boss about music (and knowing that boss, once he gets rolling talking about his favorite bands, he won't stop!).

This advice goes out to all interns. Do not talk to a boss in the middle of the work day when they are engrossed in closing deals and rallying for clients. Also, know that trying to get "in" with the top people of the company may work against you. Your supervisors, who are often closer to your age than the bosses, might find it obnoxious. Sometimes senior managers are so busy that you could do the greatest job ever and they may never remember. That doesn't make them a terrible person; it makes them a busy one.

Do the best job you can, and someone will take notice. It is more likely that you will have the longest professional relationships of your life with your direct supervisors from your internships. They are often also some of the best potential job opening resources for you, either at your current internship's company or elsewhere. The bosses will most likely retire and leave the field at some point sooner than the "youngins," not to mention the fact that bosses often rely on staff to help make hires.

Think of it this way: some people choose to treat interns terribly in general. I, on the other hand, always introduce myself to interns when I'm at meetings at other companies. Why? Hopefully to be a friendly, good person but also because I don't know who the intern is going to turn into. I already know and have a relationship with their boss and/or supervisor, that's why I'm there. I introduce myself to other companies' interns as I want to be in the loop and know who is coming up next in our field.

And soak it all up. It's important for you to learn the basic modern office skills laid out in this book, even for when you're running the show someday. For example, if you have an intern quit halfway through the semester because they are "bored" with the tasks, you better know how to FedEx or Shyp a contract. You can't skip steps, so why not enjoy the experience as you go? Similarly, you are learning and growing in every task you do and every experience you have. It is all leading to something even if it's an area of your career you did not anticipate or set out to go after.

When you're ready to get specific and narrow down your career path? Ask someone at the company you feel comfortable with if you could take them for coffee some time. Have a discussion with them about the areas within the field you are most interested in and how they feel you should work towards getting there.

But don't waste this meeting by asking how one got their start. It's perfect for an interview, but in this day and age—when I take the time out of my endless work days to meet with a student—I'm disappointed if they know nothing about me. Not because I think I'm Bill Gates and have that many achievements, but because this information already exists all over the Internet and is also present on our company's website. I don't have time to repeat myself on information that is widely available. If you have a question *about* my experience or how you can move forward on where you want to go, ask away! But please don't waste someone's time to "pick their brain" on information like how they got their start, if it is already out there and easily accessible.

Ideally, you want to be informed and prepared but conversational, all while keeping an open mind. I know, it's a lot to remember, but you'll get better at this every time you do it. With practice and time, these conversations will come with more ease.

For example, I recently had a meeting with a potential consulting client. I researched in advance the person I met with, enough that I had in the back of my mind the people we probably knew in common based on his background.

This part of the conversation arose naturally when the colleague said he used to work at RCA; to which I said, "Oh, so you must know David Bason, who signed The Dresden Dolls when he was at Roadrunner." (I also know that everyone loves Dave Bason! So this comment was a hit in the meeting.)

The book you are currently reading also came up in conversation, and the colleague, who is a CEO, was thrilled about the prospects. I told him positive stories of how nice Bason was to me when I was an intern for The Dresden Dolls. The colleague told me about his disappointment with a recent intern who quit shortly after beginning her role because she was asked to research hotels. For an event-based company (as this entity was), researching travel is actually pretty high up as far as intern tasks go.

I can't stress enough that at the end of the day, even the coolest jobs are *work*. When I was a tour manager, people always wanted to get "backstage." Guess what's backstage? People doing boring production work to make the show happen! I promise you, it's really not that exciting. So if you want to get "backstage" and work at a company that does "events," I encourage you to get *really* good at booking hotels when asked, as people often stress if travel accommodations don't go well. It's actually quite a lot of responsibility, which you can either take seriously or risk getting yelled at for seemingly petty but relevant travel errors.

WHAT YOU CAN GAIN WHEN THERE'S NOTHING TO DO

I had internships where I was given nothing to do. In those moments, I would observe. I listened to folks on the phone—not in a creepy or unprofessional manner, but for knowledge and to be aware of how people handle themselves in the workplace. What sort of manner and phrases do they use when they're on the phone? Observe how to act and listen, and learn when to speak on a conference or one-on-one call. How and when do people clock in and out for the day? How do folks present themselves online and with social media? What are they wearing as far as that field's dress code norms go? <u>There is *so* much information to pick up at an internship by observing</u> **and the vast majority of it will never be communicated directly to you.**

In short, when you need more work to do at your internship, be mindful of waiting for the right moment to ask. This generally occurs when there is an ebb in conversation or phone calls; observe calmly and you'll find the right time. Through your observations, you may find the sweet spot of doing the kind of work that helps most. Often, intern supervisors are too busy to even dole out tasks.

If you are acutely aware of what is going on around you, maybe you can see things that need to be done that you can help with. Definitely read the following chapter on "pro-activeness" with regard to asking before doing, but we're not talking about writing marketing plans here. It could be as menial as taking out the recycling. Maybe the company doesn't recycle and you could help jumpstart a recycling program.

Choosing a project in between generating marketing plans and trash disposal is optimal here. See a messy bookshelf? Ask if you can organize it! Digital files with inconsistent formatting? Same! Always ask before doing things that aren't asked of you. Use your best judgment based on what you observe of how you can contribute in a way that maybe your supervisor doesn't have time to assign you.

The point is, just do it. Do it all, no matter what the task (again, within moral and ethical reason). If you think it sucks, reevaluate the field at the end of your internship. It's equally great to figure out what turns you off professionally as well as what inspires you. But if the task seems below you, know that this is what work is. If you're not doing it, your supervisor is, and chances are, they aren't going to complain about it because they understand that's what it takes to move forward.

Ultimately, you are building your name and reputation from day one. Even before day one, when applying and interviewing. It is your name on the email address. It is you showing up in the office. Own this in a natural and genuine way. Above and beyond all, <u>DO NOT BE ABOVE ANYTHING. Ever.</u> This rule will contribute to getting you far in both your career and life. You'll learn new skills that will be useful in the long-term. There is no way I could be a successful entrepreneur without various types of basic and modern office skills, many of which I gleaned as an intern.

People will remember your hard work and positive spirit if that is what you put out to the folks around you. This will make a huge difference in both the long- and short-term, professionally and personally, and will pay dividends with regard to recommendations and future job placements.

That said (and we'll get into this more in the networking chapter), don't just do what is asked of you; do what you're told. I ask interns to arrive at 10 AM. That means 10 AM, not 9:45. If I have a breakfast meeting that runs long and I'm not getting back to the office until 9:50, you may be left out in the cold, literally. Along the same lines, I know I have until 10 AM to work without interruption, which is nothing against anyone. It just means that I blocked off that time to work on specific projects without interruption.

In general, if you are 5 minutes late for something, no one will mind. But anything longer and people will take notice, whether you're an intern or the company founder. Of course it happens to all of us from time to time. And when it does? Send the person you are meeting a text message if you have a mobile phone number (text is preferred here as they are more likely to see it) or email to let them know.

It's amazing how many times I'm complimented on this to this day, even if I am only 5 minutes or so late in the end. It frees up the other person to catch up on work on their phone or maybe enjoy a few moments in peaceful silence. Even if they don't get the message, they'll see it later and know you were on top of things and considerate of their time.

HOW TO NATURALLY ENTER THE COMPANY'S CULTURE

I truly believe that great, reliable, and consistent work speaks for itself. But we all know it does take a bit more to fully fit into a company's "culture." Let me also say that I want you to be yourself! One reason I wanted to work in the arts was to surround myself with creative types who saw no limits or boundaries. But even that is a culture, of course. So whether you are climbing the ranks in finance or are looking to join Cirque du Soleil, you are going to have to fit in at work in some form or another, which shouldn't be too unnatural as most likely you are interested in the field you are pursuing.

Start simply. As I'll continue to repeat, say yes to everything you're invited to. If you're invited to nothing? See if the most accessible/friendliest person (you feel comfortable asking) wants to get lunch sometime. If you're interning at a company where no one takes lunch breaks (a sad reality, but a reality nonetheless), ask people if you can pick up coffee for them. Create your own ways to engage.

Go to every event you can surrounding the company. We'll get into appropriate event behavior more in Chapter 9, but interact with your colleagues and network with those at other companies at events. Don't be shy to let people at other companies know that you are an intern; they were most likely an intern once too, and most folks are happy to talk about their interning experiences.

Keep an eye out for industry events and mixers. Even if the thought makes you want to run home and hide under the covers, introduce yourself to at least one person—maybe work up to trying to meet five by the end of each night as you evolve. I'll cover more on this in the networking chapter, but in order to make yourself indispensable, you have to engage; both on the receiving and giving end. Follow folks you meet on Twitter if you don't get their card. Shoot them a tweet saying it was great to meet them. If you truly can't make an event once in a while, don't be too hard on yourself! There will be another one.

Ultimately, your internship experience is what *you* make of it. You have your foot in the door. Now maximize all of the above tips and everything within this book to make the most of your experience. Even if the people around you are nice, helpful, and care about you, they do not necessarily have the time to lay out every detail. And that's great, because you're going to learn and expand your brain in ways you never even imagined by committing to all of the above and consistently obtaining skills throughout all levels of your career.

KEY TAKEAWAYS

Prepare to work extremely hard. Remember that you are at your internship to learn, but also to work. Projects are not always fun or immediately rewarding. The very definition of "work" can be downright difficult and stressful. You owe it to yourself, and your future company, to accept this fact and dive in wholeheartedly to the tasks you are assigned. Show up on time, do what is asked of you, try to be as helpful as possible, and have a good attitude while you're doing it.

Realize "timing" is everything. Learning the appropriate time and place to approach your superiors can be tricky, but you will be more successful when you carefully choose the right times to assert yourself. For example, never approach your boss for a chat in the middle of a busy workday. Instead chat them up at an industry or after work event. If you need to ask your supervisor for more tasks, wait until they are finished with their busy day or a quiet moment. Be sensitive and mindful to what's going on around you, and you'll be fine.

Build relationships with the appropriate colleagues. Don't spend your entire internship trying to impress the head of the company. The people who will take notice of your hard work are often your supervisor and the employees you directly interact with. These are the folks who will remember your keen sense of organization and attention to detail down the road—and they will often be the ones to put in a good word for you or know when job openings arise within the field.

When there's nothing "to do,"—observe to learn. Even when there's a standstill at work, there's *plenty* to learn. Pay attention to what is going on around you at all times. Listen (without being creepy) to phone calls, review every email you come across from the bottom up to get a sense of the communication styles as well as names within your industry, and notice the way employees interact with one another. You have an opportunity to walk away with a better understanding of how the company is run, so absorb all you can whenever you can.

Eight

Being "Proactive"

Asking Before Doing.

While many interns I encounter have never been given the advice to make themselves indispensable, almost all seem to be armed with the information that they should be "proactive." Although this command that they have picked up along the way is incredibly well-intentioned, in practice it rarely works. Most companies have rules and standards for reasons, and interns shouldn't attempt to shake things up unnecessarily. Don't get me wrong, if an intern suggests something that we have never thought of previously—*amazing!* And as we'll discuss below, you'll get credit in any sane circumstance. But I'll lay out how to handle your urges for proactivity.

Keep in mind that companies' best practices exist for a reason, including preventing certain scenarios from happening. When an intern does suggest something that we haven't thought of before, I am *all* over it. I will heavily credit, praise, tell colleagues, and post on the Internet what the intern has brought to the table. However, this is rarely the case. This is NOT meant to discourage you from thinking creatively or outside of the box by any means! It is more of a reminder that taking each step as it comes is important. Master each step as you go, and once you understand all angles of it, maybe you can figure out a better way to innovate your industry.

I'd rather you be the best intern possible instead of coming off as un-necessarily arrogant. Keep your place in mind. Skipping steps is rare for anyone successful, and as discussed, can hurt you in the long run if you have gaps in your professional education. So absolutely bring up ideas when appropriate, especially if you feel you have mastered what you are doing and have a better way. But know that you are more of an asset to the company by helping them with what they need to get done; not what you think needs to be done.

WHY "PROACTIVE" ISN'T THE BEST APPROACH FOR INTERNS: EXAMPLES OF INITIATIVE GONE WRONG!

I generally see well-intended intern "pro-activeness" in small, mostly harmless forms. I mention this because we're also going to highlight an extreme example of proactive behavior. But let's begin.

I had an intern who was *very* excited, rightfully so, about helping with a sponsorship campaign for a large artist at a previous internship. Awesome! It was great to talk with him about this during his interview. Regardless, his previous experience did not mean he understood the modern office basics outlined in this book, or that he had mastered other skills we had to offer.

We treat all interns the same. They start at the first level and as they master each task, they move up and on. Unfortunately, we had to hear about his previous project so often that it aimed a glaring spotlight on the fact that he wasn't responding to all messages or showing up to our team conference calls regularly.

Note that our team conference calls were intended specifically for the interns; they were otherwise not company-wide calls. That was the time when the interns could practice their conference call skills and ask me anything they wanted about the industry and their careers; questions big and small that had come up throughout the process. It was their time to get educated beyond questions oriented around daily tasks.

This particular intern showed me that he did not have the basic skills in place to respond to emails, nor did he have the initiative to show up and participate. *Nor* did a big sponsorship project via him ever land on my desk. That intern should be very proud of helping with that project at his previous internship, but it does not mean he doesn't have more to learn.

The example I just gave is a reminder to avoid behaving as if you're "above" the work of interning. It should dissuade you from believing you know more than you actually do. Smaller examples of this attitude include contacting someone outside of the company without permission, or in the entertainment industry, contacting an artist / client without permission.

These rules don't exist because the powers that be are control freaks (believe it or not!). They are there to ensure a seamless workflow for our outside vendors, partners, colleagues, and artists. The best "proactive" intentions in the world do not take away from the fact that breaking these rules affects the people on the receiving end's time and our company's relationships with these colleagues.

So when approaching any task in your internship, please ask before doing! Again, if it's a great idea, we'll tell you to run with it. 99 percent of the time, a supervisor's experience will override a well-intended reach out to someone outside of the company. While we've discussed that it's your name on the email address, it's ultimately the company's domain that you are representing. And from intern to executive, we expect a presentation of professionalism for anyone that is a part of our team.

Your intern supervisor is there for a reason. Ask them for assistance only after you've tried to complete your task with the instructions you've been given and still can't figure out the problem. Don't ever go outside or around them. When interns reach out to clients without asking, they might be asking for information that we already have on file. Imagine what the client must think of the company if we don't have information accessible that they know they have provided before.

Here's another example, taken from my industry: if you've seen someone from Spotify copied on an email that you've had access to, don't email them to update an artist's bio without asking your supervisor first. As logical and helpful as that may seem, All Music Guide handles these updates, not Spotify. By asking before doing, you'll learn the processes surrounding your industry of choice instead of upsetting your supervisor that you hit up a vice president at Spotify, who will now pay less attention to our emails when we want to pitch them something on behalf of one of our clients.

The most extreme example I've ever heard of proactivity-gone-wrong came from the president of a deeply respected publishing company. The company's cleaning person was so much a part of their working family that the president's wife would give him holiday presents each year. Until one day, the office manager wondered aloud why the cleaning person didn't show up.

She called the cleaning service to find out that their company's cleaning person had been let go by someone within the company: an intern. The intern was confronted and said he had overheard a few people saying that the cleaning person talked too much. So he took it upon himself to call the cleaning person and fire them to be "proactive."

Again, this is of course an extreme example, but it goes back to the fact that none of us are above anything or anyone. That said, as an intern, it is not your place to fire someone! The intern was asked to leave immediately and to never put that company on their résumé. Hopefully the lesson was learned—and of course, the beloved cleaning person was then reinstated.

We want you to be eager. We want you to be excited. At the same time, take a deep breath. You're there to learn, not to delegate quite yet. Take it all in and use common sense.

When in doubt, ASK! Please do not do any semi-major tasks due to your well-intentioned initiative without asking; no matter how many times "be proactive" has been drilled into your head. As exemplified above, the cliché "ask for forgiveness, not permission" does not apply here.

A far more common example of misguided initiative is interns bringing to the table whatever they think the company *should* be focusing on, instead of the tasks they are given. Via my research on the Warner Brothers' lawsuit, *Newsweek* stated, "[The intern had] been spending his downtime trying to get the A&R [Artists and Repertoire] department excited about a band that was doing well in Thailand."

Don't get me wrong, the intern in this lawsuit had some horrible disadvantages that I discovered when I looked into the case. However, A&R departments at any label, let alone a major label, are extremely busy. Everyone wants their attention. The staff needs help; they don't need more on their plate.

It's very cool that the intern tried to get the A&R department to pay attention, but continuing to assert one's personal project instead of focusing on the tasks given is something I often see. If we—leadership—need more work to do, we can take on more artists and clients. In the meantime, we generally need to complete what is in front of us first. If you're super pumped about something, pick a quiet moment to go over it with your supervisor. But do not let it take away from what you have been asked to do.

The same thing happened recently at my start-up. We were interested in having someone check our social media regularly, and instead were constantly hit with sponsorship ideas from our intern that didn't make sense for our brand (this is a different person than the previously mentioned intern who was proud of his sponsorship work).

Every moment I spent explaining that alcohol wasn't an appropriate partner for our brand, our social media wasn't getting checked the way we had asked. I ended up doing it, which was totally fine, but is kind of the opposite of asking an intern to help. Bring your idea to the table at the right time. But there is no need to bring it up over and over again if it doesn't align with the company's goals and the work at hand.

If you're *dying* to be proactive, as mentioned, don't be above taking out the recycling! That's something I did as an employee, intern, and still do now. I've had major artists who own studios that are so grateful when an intern who has been hanging around for hours picks up a broom. We know this isn't what you went to audio engineering school for, but it does help.

Studio sessions tend to consist of countless hours and a lot of waiting around. As an intern, you're there to observe, wrap cables, and learn from a master of one's craft, for sure. But a simple and harmless proactive gesture such as taking out the trash when it's full, or cleaning up in a studio or office kitchen, can go a long way and help you stand out as a thoughtful person.

A FRIENDLY WORD OF ADVICE: IF YOU HAVE A GROUNDBREAKING IDEA, PROTECT IT

If you do have an idea or business model that you believe is truly groundbreaking, put it down in private digital form. Share it with family or even an attorney if you happen to know one. Bring it up to your boss at the right moment, but have it documented elsewhere in advance.

If an intern came to me with an incredible new concept, I would shine the light on them like crazy to make the idea happen. Either way, it's a cut-throat world, and if your idea is business or world-changing, protecting yourself is important. Take the above precautions and maybe throw on your Twitter: *Presenting a new idea to my boss today, can't wait!* to publicly document your actions without giving away the farm. Hopefully all bosses will work with you for your idea to come to fruition. Just in case, the above tips are there to protect you.

Above and beyond all, have faith that if you are consistently doing your tasks well and are reliable, people will notice. Focus on that more so than being "proactive" and you'll get further in the long-run, faster.

KEY TAKEAWAYS

Make yourself indispensable. Somewhere along the line, interns and students have been told they should be "proactive." But proactivity isn't necessarily the best goal when you haven't yet learned the ropes at your internship or industry at large. Instead of taking work matters into your own hands and potentially causing unintended harm, focus on becoming an indispensable part of the team.

Remember, you're there to learn. Keep in mind that you don't already know everything about your field, and the way to get to know everything is by doing. The purpose of an internship is to learn skills and immerse yourself in a new industry. Admit to yourself that you *could* learn to compose a stronger email, that you could improve your interpersonal skills, or that you're really not as familiar with modern office software as you could be. Then resolve to keep learning new things each day and become the best intern, and eventually, best candidate for the workforce you can be, and on to the best employee possible and upwards! There is plenty to master, so stay optimistic, humble, and get to work.

Ask before doing! Prior to taking any action outside of your agreed upon tasks, check with your supervisor first. It is far better to double-check with an experienced employee than risk making a judgement call that damages the company, brand and your personal reputation. Always, always, ask a question when you want to do something outside of your tasks to avoid a potential mistake.

To be safe, document your original ideas. There are some ruthless people in the world, so it's a good idea to safeguard your ideas before sharing them. If you have an idea you are confident will innovate an industry or even the company you're at, protect it by putting it in private digital form and consider having a lawyer look it over as well. Also, consider giving a social media shout-out hinting that you're sharing your big idea with your boss. It's much better to be safe than risk having your idea stolen! At the same time, we rarely see ideas stolen, so don't go unnecessarily having folks sign NDAs either.

Nine

Authentic Networking in Your Field and What NOT to Do.

+Building YOUR Professional Brand Online and Off.

The concept of "networking" has always been an odd word for me, since I have a natural curiosity about people. This intrigue heightened when I was coming up in my career, as I loved meeting others in my field. That said, "networking" is intimidating to many people, and even more so now, when we spend more time looking at screens than interacting with humans throughout our lives.

Over the past few years, I've been asked to participate on panels about networking. Initially, I thought it was kind of a silly topic. In reality, these were some of my most packed speaking engagements ever! Clearly, there is a need for this knowledge.

PROFESSIONAL NETWORKING: WHO, WHAT, WHEN, WHERE, WHY...HOW?

Whether you are a shy person or not, start locally. Many universities offer networking events and mixers throughout the year. There is no better way to begin building your network than by connecting with fellow students around you, especially if you are studying the same field.

*At networking events, go forth, introduce yourself, and have fun.
A great ice breaker in any situation is to ask where someone is
from. It should at least get the ball rolling for you.*

If you happen to be near a city with professional networking events, definitely go! Many of these events are public across industries. In my field there is a free monthly "Music Industry Mixer" put on by Jenn Federici in NYC. Similarly, NY Tech Meetup is a great group that puts on a monthly event for $10. Research your career field and see what's out there.

If you want to take your networking pursuits to the next level, you can check out industry conferences. Know that these can be *very* expensive. Look into your university's programs to ascertain if they offer grants to send students to events such as Austin's South by Southwest. I attended my first SXSW while in college and encourage others to do so if you can.

It's great to immerse yourself into an overwhelming situation like SXSW when you're an intern, instead of being flung into it as a young professional. By then you'll have some experience under your belt on how to best handle these situations, instead of going in green at entry-level like most others.

Whether you are introverted or not, my attorney has a great rule of thumb for networking events: she always tries to leave with at least five business cards. To that same point, print up cards for yourself! Surprisingly, it's an antiquated form of networking that has yet to go away. Particularly when at large industry events with a ton of people, it can be great to go through the cards when you return and remember all of the people you met.

In general, if you are targeting relatively high-level people, do your research on commonalities you might have. Are they a big Boston Red Sox fan? Do they practice yoga? Are they from Wisconsin? Do they love elite swimming as much as I do? There are so many things to talk about besides work.

I've always felt that it's not stalking if the information is there. At the same time, use your judgment and pick out a few nuggets. This might give you an in, as opposed to just talking about work, as even the most successful people in the coolest industries get sick of talking about work and have interests outside of their job.

One of my favorite things about networking is how it has blended seamlessly into social media. It's called social "networking" for a reason. When you do return from an event with a stack of business cards, you can email those whom it makes sense to connect with or, when you're further along, have business to do with.

For more passive networking, you can follow folks on Twitter or add them on LinkedIn. Following people on Twitter is a great way to communicate after you've heard an impressive presentation. If it's an in-demand speaker who was swept out the door after their speech, shooting them a tweet to let them know how much you enjoyed their talk can go a long way.

As mentioned, most people, especially busy and fancy folks, get way too many emails. Reaching out cold to ask someone if you may buy them coffee to "pick their brain" works once in a while. However, they are most likely extremely busy, in demand, and don't need another email. Tweeting at someone you've seen speak is a more fun and seamless way to connect and network if it's a "bigger" person. I don't want to discourage you from reaching out to your dream people; more so, I want to help you get results from these reach-outs.

BUILDING YOUR BRAND THROUGH PREPARATION

To that same point, start building your "brand" online as early as possible. As cheesy as that sounds, it's important. I once had a high-level colleague ask me to dinner to discuss how he could better "brand" himself, as he was impressed with how I had branded myself. I laughed aloud, as there was never any forethought behind my internet presence. Save for one thing: I have a personal rule of only posting positive things on the Internet.

When you follow this rule of thumb, you really can't go wrong. I started a Twitter account in 2008, almost sarcastically thinking to myself "Maybe someone will care about a young woman starting a company." Within a few years *Billboard* named me a "must executive to follow" on Twitter, two years in a row. Shortly after, they put my name on the cover.

Other executives asked who my publicist was. I didn't have one. Instead I prepared diligently for panels and speaking engagements. Just as many folks don't prepare, so my preparation caused me to stand out in one way or another. More panels and speaking engagements followed. Eventually *Billboard* writers picked up on our modern business tactics, with the editor at the time finally saying to me at a conference in Europe: "You are *everywhere!*"

Little me did all of that without a conscious "brand" in mind other than staying positive and being genuine online, as well as doing the best job possible at all events I was asked to attend. You'd be amazed how every little action adds up in the long run.

THE POWER OF "YES": WHY YOU SHOULD ATTEND EVERY INDUSTRY EVENT YOU CAN

We've discussed "saying yes to everything." This is mostly with regard to events. If you are invited to a company or industry event—go! If you get there and don't see anyone you know, don't be shy, no matter how hard it is. Turn to the person next to you and introduce yourself. Then ask them what they do and/or where they work. Take it from there. They are there to network too and may be equally terrified to strike up a conversation, and relieved when you do.

At the same time, working in a "cool" and busy field such as entertainment can also yield high pressure and in-demand events that interns want to attend. Hopefully you are invited to help out, but if not, find a quiet moment to ask if you can help out at the event. If the answer is yes, find a way to help out while you're there if you're not given specific tasks via all of the tips you've already read about for in-office help during lulls.

I was super bummed when I asked an intern if she could help with an artist's merchandise at a Mumford & Sons' event. When she arrived, the first thing she asked me was how long she had to be there for. Not for any particular reason, as that would have been fine. It instead came across as though she couldn't wait to leave.

When I brought this up in her review, she expressed that she wanted to be hanging out with the people I was with at the show. I explained to her that it was a Tuesday night, I was exhausted, and couldn't wait to go home and go to bed. The people surrounding me were in similar boats. I got to know those people by helping at merch tables over the years and cultivating relationships; not asking how soon I could leave.

Attitude can truly be everything; keep that in mind at work and net-working events. If you ask to help at an event and the answer is no, don't be bummed. Oftentimes there really is limited room at the event and it simply is what it is. But know that your offering of help will not go unno-ticed for the future.

Similarly, I had a respected artist friend who was not on our roster contact me once, as she was opening for a pretty big band at Webster Hall in New York. She asked if there were any interns who could help with her merch. When I asked around, everyone responded with, "How much?"

I knew this artist would probably pay, but I really didn't want to bug her about it. As I'd been planning on attending the show anyway, I told her I'd happily help with the merch. She said, "Really?" knowing that I was a partner at our firm. I ended up meeting David Byrne at the merch table, reconnected with the head of Merge Records, had a great view of the show, and was offered cash from the artist for helping her out (which I turned down) but accepted a beer or two from her instead and enjoyed the music.

Bummer for the interns who turned down the gig. They didn't get those experiences, contacts, and chose to stay home instead. I can't stress enough that by saying "yes" to everything I was invited to for the first decade of my career or so is how I know endless folks within my field.

TO DRINK OR NOT TO DRINK: (WHAT WAS THE QUESTION??)

Getting offered a beer at an industry event brings up the topic of drinking. I was offered my first drink at 19, during a work event as an intern, by a boss. I truly had *no idea* what to do.

In reality, the professional thing is to turn down the drink, no matter what your age. Don't get me wrong; getting drinks, dinner, etc. is part of networking for sure. At the same time, I love spending SXSW sober while I watch colleagues embarrass themselves by drinking too much at out-of-office work events.

Have a drink or two when you're of age if you want, alternate it with water, and avoid day drinking at events at all costs. You'll gain a reputation for having your collective shit together in professional, off-site situations, instead of being an industry drunk. If you dig alcohol, enjoy it with your friends! Outside of work situations.

Above all, remember that whether you're networking at your school or at a major industry event, you are putting yourself out there. Be responsible for your actions, be kind, genuine, have fun, do the things you say you'll do, and follow up. Repeat this networking cycle, and keep going until, like me, you know too many industry people!

SOCIAL MEDIA: A PRESSURE-FREE WAY TO STAY IN TOUCH

Facebook has been a great tool for me to stay in touch with work folks and it's great for posting content on our clients. That said, LinkedIn is a safer professional bet and Twitter is even less pushy. So use your judgment, and use all of these great tools to stay in touch with the new colleagues you are meeting along the way at your internship and beyond.

After you've been at an internship for a few weeks, feel free to add folks on Facebook that you have a good rapport with. Once in a while someone might shoot you a message letting you know they don't add work folks to their Facebook, which is totally fine. Don't be offended. But otherwise, assuming all of your posts have been positive throughout the years, this is a great way to stay in touch with people both during and after your internship. That way they can see what you're up to and vice versa.

Many people change jobs within their field throughout their careers. The people you meet at your internship(s) are going to spread their wings. As of this writing, Facebook can be a great way to keep track and see where everyone lands, which can help you and vice versa in the long run.

Final obvious pro tip: *Do not* complain about your boss, internship, or supervisor on social media. I saw a publicist post that an intern did this. Use some common sense. If you're having a terrible experience, we've discussed ways to address this. Unfortunately, social media is not the place to do so.

I'm a naturally outgoing person who loves talking to people. But the idea of networking initially terrified me as an intern. I had an accent (Midwestern), the regimented lifestyle of a jock, I came from what many would consider to be the opposite culture of rock 'n' roll, and I knew no one—literally *no one*—in the music industry when I began. Well, technically my parents were good friends with the couple who owned the music store in town, and they go to a big industry conference every year and are quite connected. That said, even industry conferences used to intimidate me initially.

My point is, no matter how shy you are, you can break through this apprehension surrounding networking. In fact, most of the shy students I know often have an advantage by being aware that this is something they need to work on, and by understanding that networking is an asset to their career. It has been my more naturally shy colleagues and business partners who have given me these insights. Although they were in awe of my outgoing personality, they taught me that hanging out isn't fun (in any way) for them in most cases. It's work, and it is a key part of building your professional reputation and career.

KEY TAKEAWAYS

Show up for as many events as you can. Part of networking happens by simply "being there," so attend events within your industry often. Say yes anytime the opportunity to help out presents itself, and do show enthusiasm while you assist in any way possible. You never know who you might meet or what opportunities might arise.

Keep your wits about you. Drinking is generally a bad idea at work / work events, though it is an accepted aspect of networking. But you don't want to have regrets or embarrassment after a night of sloppy behavior so be careful (and be of age!). If you choose to imbibe at company or industry events, do so with great moderation and have water in between (maximum two) alcoholic beverages.

Use social media to stay in touch. Twitter, Facebook, and LinkedIn are fantastic ways to network without seeming pushy. Use Twitter to communicate with high-level figures, and keep in touch with closer colleagues through Facebook and LinkedIn. Be sure to keep your online profiles professional and positive.

Above all, realize networking is a skill. Don't be dismayed if you do not think you are a strong networker right now. Practice will definitely improve your game. At industry events, take a deep breath and introduce yourself to someone. Classic icebreakers like "Where are you from?" go a long way. You'll be amazed how much easier it becomes after a few tries.

Ten

Overwhelmed?

Take a Deep Breath and Take Care of Yourself—It Will Make You a Better Worker and Person.

Work-life balance is a more prevalent topic than ever. Yet as Americans, we still aren't great at it. As many companies offer to cover gym memberships or even provide on-site yoga or meditation, health is becoming more and more of a priority in workforces across the globe.

In my early twenties, I regularly pulled all-nighters. Now? I sleep 9 hours a night! If something needs to get taken care of on a weekend, I will take care of it, no doubt. At the same time, I've grown to prioritize my health, which not only enhances my life but enhances my work performance.

CREATE & BUILD HEALTHY HABITS NOW

Developing healthy habits while in college and in your twenties is crucial. As a college athlete, I worked out the day after my last championship meet, not wanting to get "out of shape." But as an American child of the "no pain, no gain" 1980s, exercise seemed like a chore.

In the modern era, we tend to know better. Taking care of oneself enhances all areas of life. I know that when I go on retreats, prioritize sleep, eat healthy, drink plenty of water, skip coffee and alcohol, and exercise every day, it puts me in a better position to be at the top of my game in a variety of ways. (Every time coffee is mentioned in this book, I ordered tea. To me, "getting coffee" is a phrase that refers to a more casual and usually shorter meeting, than, say, meeting over a meal.)

Do not feel overwhelmed by this chapter. It has taken years of personal evolution to get to the lifestyle I have now. That evolution has been towards "healthful living," not "trying to be healthy." I am now at the point where being active every day isn't a chore; it's pure joy. Because much of this chapter might feel daunting or boring, it's worth it to pick and choose a tip or two here to implement into your life. Regardless, don't feel like you have to live up to a strict regimen consisting of the tenets laid out in this chapter. The people around you may thank you and you may end up thanking yourself—as all of the health choices I share here are motivated by having the most focused, clear, and energetic mind and body possible.

These guidelines point to a proven way to thrive and, frankly, get ahead of others if that is a goal. While others might be hungover, you will experience clarity of mind as you not only get things done, but enhance your brain to get as far as possible. Of course, do feel free to indulge once in a while when your body warrants it. I happen to be editing this chapter on a cold and rainy Sunday afternoon. The grilled cheese I ordered for lunch felt great and warmed me up. Remember to take everything in moderation; not depriving yourself is key.

SLEEP IS SACRED; MAKE SURE YOU'RE GETTING ENOUGH

My absolute number one health priority, above and beyond both physical activity and eating healthy, is sleep. As a teenager, whenever people would ask how I was doing, the answer was always the same: "Tired."

Yes, I was getting up crazy early for swim practice, but even on the days that I wasn't, waking up after staying up doing homework never felt natural to me. I went on retreat in Southeast Asia in my mid-twenties and slept a ton. There, I realized that I'd basically been sleep deprived my entire life. We come from a culture that often considers sleeping or naps to be a sign of laziness. Why do we deprive ourselves of something that every human clearly needs?

This concept hit home even further a few years ago when I was watching my client, multi-time Olympic gold medalist Anthony Ervin, speak to a group of exercise physiology students. One student asked about his recovery regimen. Anthony responded that sleep and naps were crucial for him. I was in the audience and could hear a few snickers from the kids in the back, as again the assumption was that sleep is tied to laziness.

Anthony continued explaining that if he doesn't get enough sleep, his body gains fat and loses muscle. He literally needs the recovery from sleep to repair and maintain the strength he has built up in training. As Anthony spoke about this, I was instantly reminded that our bodies are repairing our minds as well when we sleep. Therefore, I wondered, was it worth it when I push myself to wake up really early and deprive myself of the sleep I need?

I realize that not everyone is in the position to sleep a full night. I hesitate to even bring this topic up around my friends and colleagues with kids. That said, I have to assert that choosing to make sleep my first and foremost health priority has enhanced so many other areas of my life, that I'm now getting more done with improved physical and mental health across the board.

In my twenties, I used to be okay sleep-wise on Mondays and Tuesdays. I would be dragging by Wednesdays, tired by Thursdays, and utterly useless on Fridays. Then I'd spend most of my weekends catching up on sleep.

Not only did this cycle feel inefficient, it was a waste of time. I was sleeping away the weekends, which basically meant I was working all the time since my off-time felt wasted on catching up on sleep.

A few years ago, I realized I needed 9 hours of sleep a night. This magic number is a little different for everyone and can be easily calculated by seeing how long you generally sleep without an alarm on vacations (most likely after a few days of sleep catch-up of course). I wish I only needed 7 or 8 hours of sleep, but I need more. No wonder I was constantly exhausted as a teenager.

I have now made the decision to sleep 9 hours a night, no matter what. This amount sounds insane to most people; one colleague of mine said, "You're sleeping the whole day away!" Either way, by putting some thought into my sleep and overall schedule, sleeping 9 hours a night has truly changed my life.

No longer am I crashing by Wednesday and catching up with long naps on weekends. I now have relatively even levels of energy every day. I am just as efficient, no matter the day of the week. Of course mental burnout from too much work happens regardless. Later we'll discuss ways to take care of burnout. But thinking about your sleep, planning for it, and taking care of yourself can change you, your life, your career, and give you an edge in a multitude of ways.

Sleep is now my fuel. I ensure my 9 hours happen before speaking engagements as well as every Sunday night, so I'm fresh and ready to go on Mondays to start the week. Even when I wake up before the 9 hours, I stay in bed with my eyes closed to rest. I kid you not; I literally watch my brain solve problems and prepare for the tasks ahead that day.

It's clear that as we sleep, chemicals are being released that help our mental agility, moods, interactions with others, creativity, memory, and jumpstart ideas. For more, check out NIH.gov and search for "sleep."

Getting optimal sleep takes planning. And naps are okay to help make up for sleep! But try to make up for missing sleep that same day, or the next, to avoid building up too much debt.

DON'T LET BOOZE (OR CAFFEINE AND SUGAR) RUIN YOUR ZZZ'S

Pay attention to how alcohol affects your sleep. A nightcap might knock you out at first, but ultimately results in much less restful sleep throughout the night.

Avoid sugar and caffeine in the evenings or even consider quitting caffeine altogether. It may sound like I'm asking you to miss out on "fun," but in reality, my life is so enhanced by feeling great and refreshed every day; I wouldn't have it any other way.

You may be able to "get by" on just a few hours' sleep in your twenties, but play around with getting plenty of sleep and see what happens. You may be surprised by the results. I hope this advice helps you become even more indispensable at your internships and aids making common sense decisions, both big and small. You might even create a habit that will benefit you for life.

PRIORITIZE AN EXERCISE THAT RESONATES

Following sleep, my next health priority is exercise. Believe it or not, as a swimmer who trained all the time, a fitness-heavy lifestyle can actually lead to sloth-like behavior of just wanting to relax and eat.

Some athletes are *pure athletes* and love working out from day one, but many of us aren't. Vinyasa yoga is something I was drawn to following my college swimming years. The idea of going from swimming miles a day to a routine confined to a humble foam mat was intriguing. Not to mention the fact that the activity was actively non-competitive. We were specifically told *not* to look around at what others were doing, to instead focus on ourselves and our practice. That sure was a different attitude than growing up in a sport where ultimately the goal is to get your hand on the wall first.

Yoga's benefits on one's work-life are numerous. At my first job out of college, I was working hard. The partners and artists liked me and were appreciative of my work. Yet at the same time, there was a clique of people at the company who had known each other for years and seemed to go out of their way to not include me.

I was stunned that people in their thirties would go around and ask what everyone wanted to order for lunch but me. It was bizarre and disappointing to see such juvenile behavior as an adult. At the same time, I'd go to yoga after work and hear teachers remind us that even when people are unkind, they are still someone's daughter, brother, friend, girlfriend, sister, family member, and more. By looking at my hostile co-workers this way, I was able to view them from a genuine place of peace.

For example, I offered to pick them up coffee, truly from a good place and not in a passive-aggressive manner. The result? Those folks are now my dear friends and close colleagues. Not only did finding yoga enhance my mind and body to make me feel calm, focused, and great at work, it helped to improve my relationships with my colleagues. As well as of course numerous personal benefits that have resulted from my practice.

Eventually I found a way to get back in the water, via a family member asking if I'd do the swimming leg on a relay triathlon. I hadn't swum in years and looked at the daunting Westchester Sound with nerves. What was I getting myself into? I knew pools with lane lines, not an open body of water with waves and people all around.

As soon as I was in the water, it was like nothing had changed from my years in the pool. I knew exactly what I was doing, yet loved the challenge of a new environment. The idea of masters swimming never appealed to me as I'd been there, done that, as far as pool training went. But discovering something I was good at—that was fresh and new—was amazing.

I eventually did quite a few races around the Statue of Liberty and Governors Island, under the Brooklyn Bridge, and in the Hudson River via an organization called NYC Swim. My point is, look around, as there are *so* many ways to stay active, have fun, and do something new; physical activity can be something you grow to learn and enjoy, not dread. People in a park near my home play their own version of "Quidditch." The benefits that exercise brings to my work performance are countless, and I rarely start my day without some sort of physical activity to jumpstart the morning (or else I go after work, as exercise is also great for decompressing).

Keep fitness simple; don't overthink it or feel you have to spend a ton of money to get in physical movement. I've been a member of the New York Parks Department for years, whose fees to join their pools and gyms are $2/month if you are under the age of 24 (and not very expensive for the rest of us).

I love to bike for transportation in the warmer months, and even take conference calls while walking to and from meetings or over the Williamsburg Bridge. Yoga to the People is a studio in various cities that is donation based. There are countless free yoga classes on the Internet for when I'm traveling, and when all else fails, I try to get a good walk in while also clearing my mind.

You don't have to be an Olympic athlete or kill yourself at the gym to benefit from exercise. When I swim in pools now, I enjoy easy laps. I'm not training, nor does it feel like I'm working out. I'm moving my body to enhance how it, and my mind, feels. Again, selfishly, it contributes to making me a better worker and person.

I've discussed sleep and exercise with interested interns, and despite their youth and vigor, all who try it out see the benefits. I remember when Melissa and her friend Katie were interning for me and they were all about Insanity and Shaun T. Every day they'd come in and say, "Whoa, Shaun T kicked our butts today." Both young women enjoyed the short workouts that they could do on their own time and thrived at school and work in part because of it.

Here's another suggestion: Get moving with your co-workers! See if anyone wants to go to a yoga class, try indoor rock climbing, play the aforementioned Quidditch together, or join an industry flag football or ultimate frisbee team. It's a great way to bond and develop teamwork skills with your co-workers, and have everyone feeling great at the same time.

Meanwhile, fitness and healthy physicality continues to show up in the workplace. It's not a surprise to me that attention to posture and standing desks are now commonplace. Even more so, step counters (many of which exist already for free on smartphones) can be a great way to track being active if you truly cannot find a physical activity that appeals to you.

On days where I really need some extra energy or breaks, I love doing sun salutations (see an example here: https://www.youtube.com/watch?v=73sjOu0g58M) in between each task to help focus and stay on track. Keep a water bottle with you at all times to feel refreshed and hydrated. Choose that over soda, and it will change your health and life.

Be aware that Sunday is the day before Monday, and plan your activities with this in mind. Drink in moderation while watching football games or at brunch, or see how it feels to skip it. You'll be amazed by how great you feel at work the next day when you take care of yourself on Sundays.

It's not that I haven't enjoyed these experiences; it's that I eventually got sick of how I felt afterwards or the next day. I love using all of the tools in this chapter to feel great the majority of the time instead of repairing my health after drinking on Sundays, which ultimately is a weeknight.

EAT AND DRINK HEALTHILY

And of course, nutrition. Most people know this, but you truly are what you eat. I have noticed that I gain the most energy, no doubt, by shopping at and preparing food from my local organic farmers' market each week. It's also way cheaper than anything at any grocery store.

I love making green smoothies in the morning, eating whole grains and lean proteins throughout the day, and staying hydrated. Most people know what they need to eat—or not eat—to maximize their energy, but I wanted to mention these tips as a reminder. I certainly don't deny myself when it comes to food. I listen to what my body needs instead of what my eyes want.

Equally important, as your career evolves to the level where you're taking lunch meetings, be aware of what drags you down or uplifts you. A heavy pasta or even a large sandwich may not lead to a great afternoon of work. Try rice-based dishes for staying full; they boost my afternoons by helping me stay energized and efficient. Also, try a quick meditation before you settle back in for the day, instead of that second cup of coffee.

MEDITATE FOR SERENITY AND CLARITY

This leads me to my final health key to success: meditation. Meditation is something that has been around me most of my life, but I didn't really pay attention until my twenties. More than anything in this book, don't overthink meditation; keep it simple, because it *is* simple.

If you can find a teacher, meditation group, or online course, awesome. But if you'd like to give it a shot on your own, try sitting up straight, closing your eyes, and focusing on your breath for a minute. Achieve that and you have meditated!

Almost all meditations are based on a "single-pointed" lineage. This can be focusing on your breath, any one of your five senses, or a mantra as your single point. After you have mastered your minute, try doing 2 minutes the next day. Then 3, 4, and work up to 5 or more. See if you can do any amount of meditation daily and notice what happens.

I've had the absolute pleasure of going on 10-day silent Vipassana meditation retreats with master teachers. But even after these incredibly life-changing experiences, the right fit for me is generally meditating for 5 minutes during breaks throughout the day. I do so before big calls, meetings, or even prior to composing an important message. And I certainly meditate throughout large projects like sitting down and writing this book!

On retreat one year in Southeast Asia, I happened to meet one of the founders of PayPal. Like many others on the year-end retreat, he was there to de-stress and decompress from the year. He did so by finding places to meditate to let all of his work and life stress go. I brought up how I love to meditate before major work and life events, as it helps me to prepare and ease through these experiences. This blew his mind. He had only thought about meditation as a cure, not as a way to enhance our life in advance of potentially stressful events.

Regardless, I don't know anyone who has tried meditation on a regular basis and not enjoyed it. Similar to many of the tips in this chapter, don't get too ambitious when you start out. If you can work up to 5-minute doses, it can truly enhance your life. Selfishly, too much of my meditation practice is motivated by the idea of making me great at work. But I am always grateful for meditation in times of stress and confusion, or even just to calm down and gain perspective. It has of course simultaneously enhanced my life in many ways beyond work.

I'll end on meditation by saying this: As a young music manager, I used to wake up and feel incredibly overwhelmed by all I had to do for our artists; I wouldn't even know where to begin. Yet when I would meditate, without even trying, my brain would calm down and organize what I needed to do that day—literally putting the tasks of what needed to be done in order of priority. I would open my eyes and feel incredibly focused and have a clear plan of how to accomplish everything we were setting out to do each busy day.

This is a joy I can practice in the comfort of my home, on the subway en route to a meeting, even hiding in a bathroom if need be! Try it. Meditation is so simple, yet powerful. Again, don't overthink it. When thoughts enter your mind, just return your focus to your breath.

Above and beyond all, despite my selfish motivations to be great at work with the above tips, it's truly important to find activities that fulfill you outside of work. I hate to say it, but this will also make you a better worker! Don't get me wrong; it's important to be balanced. But if you're as Type-A or motivated as I am, these habits can greatly enhance your career, as well as your life.

Now that my energy levels are the same every day, I have to remind myself to take breaks during nights and weekends sometimes, even when

I feel great. Not only is this of course enjoyable, but it makes me that much better during the next work day. I love taking breaks on weekends and nights to be with friends and family, practice yoga, and recharge for the following work day.

Additionally, I want to share some real-world thoughts on health and business by a dear mentor of mine, Elizabeth Freund, who has been Ringo Starr's publicist and close professional confidant for thirty years. Elizabeth states:

> As a publicist, my work is highly deadline oriented, which can inspire a sense of urgency and anxiety. If I am not mindful, it's easy to give in to the feeling that there are not enough hours in each day. Although rushing from task to task gives the appearance of productivity, I have found that when I skip meals and don't take time to meditate or relax, I actually become less productive, make more mistakes, and enjoy my work less.
>
> It may seem counter-intuitive, but I feel my best when I take the extra time to take care of myself. My daily regimen includes eating healthfully (I am a vegetarian); practicing two 20-minute meditations (I do transcendental meditation first thing in the morning and in the evening); spending time outdoors, walking my dog, or even swinging on a swing to enhance my energy and spirit; and enjoying a favorite sport or class.
>
> This has had the amazing effect of giving me a broader sense of time, a steadier sense of calm, and has made me more productive, creative, and effective at my work. Most importantly, I am happier. I can more readily appreciate all aspects of my life, including my career, when I nurture my body, mind, and spirit.

Incorporating any or all of these tips will not only make you the best possible intern you can be, but you will also ultimately enjoy a better quality of life for you and those around you. Not to mention that people like

Elizabeth look great doing it! These health tips have physical benefits in addition to the positive mental and work-related aspects.

Ultimately, these tips are also there for you for when you *do* burn out, be it in the short- or long-term. If you experience burnout symptoms as an intern, you not only run the risk of making big mistakes at work, but you also won't get the most out of the experience you've been working so hard towards. Staying healthy will help avoid burnout, but on the days and times in life when it does come, you will know how to best handle it, unplug, and recharge.

I love to work and care about getting things done, no doubt. But I care about your health, happiness, and sanity above and beyond all. These tips will help you thrive in your internships. They will keep you healthy while you work hard and de-stress you after long days, so you can tackle each new day feeling refreshed, focused, and ready to go.

KEY TAKEAWAYS

Develop your work-life balance. Do yourself a favor and try to achieve a sustainable work-life balance early on. This will serve you well throughout your career, as your work will shine brightest when you are healthy and happy. Pursue mental, physical, and spiritual wellness and not only will you feel better, but your performance will increase as well.

Prioritize sleep. Without getting the proper amount of rest, you can't give your all to any area of life. Figure out how much rest you need, and structure your life so you're able to get those crucial nightly hours of shut-eye. Don't shy away from naps either, as they can restore you when you've fallen behind on your rest.

Make peace with exercise. Find a workout that you like, and try to approach exercise from a place of fun, joy and/or enthusiasm. It doesn't have to be painful and exhausting! If you're looking for something low impact and accessible (that still yields impressive results!), give yoga a try. It is incredibly grounding and can be practiced anywhere.

Feed your mind and body with quality food. A healthy diet consisting of fresh veggies, hearty proteins, and wholesome grains will get you through the most hectic workday. Visit a local organic farmers' market for high-quality foods at affordable prices. And when you're making your lunch selections at work, be wary of carb-heavy entrées that will make you sluggish and tired for the rest of the day. Instead choose a lighter fare like rice based dishes that will give you energy without the crash.

Try meditation. Meditation helps you handle the sometimes overwhelming pressures of work and life. It deepens your connection to the present moment and helps you find a sense of calm in a chaotic world. Take time to meditate at least once a day (more if you can manage it), and notice how your inner and outer world changes. Chances are it will become a tool you can call upon anytime for instant peace and clarity.

Eleven

Finish Strong

How to Stay in Touch for Maximum Benefits.

You've made it! Almost :).

Just about every great intern I've ever had, even the best of the best, dropped the ball at the tail end of their internships. It is completely understandable to get overwhelmed and excited when graduation or another opportunity is on the horizon and quickly approaching. But think about it - the business world does not slow down or stop just because the end or a new beginning is happening for you.

As you've seen and learned, the "real world" does not operate on the semester system. In this chapter, we'll remind you how to wrap-up and finish strong to leave a great impression on the folks you interned for moving forward, to thereby receive maximum benefits.

You have put in hours of time over many months while building a great reputation and rapport with your intern supervisors, as well as with the company overall. Now, more than ever, is the time *not* to drop the ball. As your schedule and life starts to shift into graduation or back-to-school mode, try to stick to whatever practices you've culled from this book and your experience to get where you are now. And don't stop!

HOW TO COMPLETE YOUR INTERNSHIP THE RIGHT WAY AND WHERE TO GO FROM HERE

I should know better by now, but I'm always stunned when interns at all levels flake out the last few weeks of an internship. While you've learned at your internship that mistakes happen, you also know that at school, you can't flat out skip class or not turn in assignments for the final few weeks.

The same rules apply here. There is no such thing as "senioritis" in the business world (or maybe there is; I guess it's okay for people about to retire to get a case of senioritis! I think we can all agree they deserve it at that point). One way to solidify a lasting great impression, on top of all the wonderful work you've done, is to <u>finish strong</u>. Again, note that almost every intern does *not* finish strong, which means this is an awesome and relatively easy way to stand out.

I recently asked an intern at the end of his time with us, when would be a good time to set up a call for a review and to give career advice. I took the time to follow up a few times and never heard back.

That is of course an extreme example, but I've also asked interns to give me a report of what they've worked on, which has not always been completed. I wanted to use that report to discuss what they learned and what we both can improve upon, while ensuring that all tasks had been completed.

There is nothing worse in the day-to-day modern business world than radio silence. It's always tough to see the truly great interns drop the ball at the end of their internships. Nothing will take away from your loyalty and diligence throughout the semester, but it's a bummer way to wrap up either way.

The flipside, and here is a time where you absolutely should be proactive, is to ask your supervisor if there is anything you *can* do to help wrap-up your time with the company. Create a list of regular tasks you worked on, as well as a how-to guide for those tasks that can be shared with future interns. Offer to be available a month or so after your internship, if possible, for the next intern, who may have questions that come up.

Your supervisor might not only be relieved for this respite, but also impressed about the truly helpful initiative you are taking. Initiative works best when it helps to move things forward (with permission in an intern's case), as opposed to asking how you can help. Don't fear asking, but keep this in mind at all levels of business. Figure out how to contribute instead of asking how to contribute (but again, if you're an intern, ask first before executing on your initiative and intention to help!).

This should go without saying, and most interns are great about it, but it's worth pointing out: If your supervisor contacts you with a question on locating a file or something you worked on after your internship, answer them! You can not only take that opportunity to engage and stay in touch with the company, but it will be greatly appreciated. So much so that when you are in job-hunt mode, those details and actions will help your prospects even more.

Say you've finished strong (thank you!) and your internship does not have a lost file they need to contact you about. What is the best way to stay in touch, both for job prospects and networking benefits?

I was happily surprised shortly after an intern from my start-up wrapped up and I received a physical thank-you note in the mail. It was such a kind and thoughtful, yet simple, gesture. Sending a gift is great, but of course not required. A handwritten thank-you note is something that costs little money and goes a long way in an otherwise digital world.

Do your due diligence on following and adding the rest of the staff on Twitter, LinkedIn, and Facebook (assuming you deem Facebook to be appropriate for your field); you should now have a collection of virtual contacts for your burgeoning network. If you haven't engaged with folks online yet in this manner, now is a great time. Even for that shy person in the corner whom you didn't get to know all that well. They are now part of your network and you are part of theirs.

If you are graduating soon and about to enter the workforce, reach out to your supervisor and others you are comfortable with at the company to see if they have time to discuss your career prospects either at the company, in the field, or in general. If it's a great company and you truly enjoyed your experience, let them know you'd be happy to help any time and would love to know about any future openings.

If it's the kind of office where a lot of folks are coming in and out from other companies, it may be worth your time to offer to be there a day or a few hours a week while you job hunt. It will increase your odds of being in the "right place at the right time," while continuing to be out in the real world/professional field instead of applying cold online while at home. You never know who you'll meet coming in and out of the office, and how that can benefit you now as well as in the future.

Either way, check in every few months or so just to say hello. Ask your internship colleagues to keep you in mind for anything they hear of, or just see if they want to catch a show (in the music industry), a baseball game, or a yoga class—anything you've connected with your colleagues on previously. And continue to go to public work events.

I had a former intern show up at an industry showcase I was hosting, only to tell her that my business partner was executive producing a new TV show and they were hiring. Seeing Kelsey at the show reminded me to tell her that and she was hired by the show shortly after. Showing up can make all the difference in the world.

In general, stay in touch respectfully. Don't email every day or week. Re-tweet and share relevant posts from the company or key coworkers. This will show that you are interested and engaged in your field even after your internship. Get creative in your communications with the places you interned, and you will stand out.

I'm usually able to place interns when they do stay in touch, as I'm then reminded when I have or hear of a job opening to share with them.

Not to mention that boss types talk amongst ourselves! When openings arise, we often ask each other for intern recommendations to hire before ever posting jobs publicly.

You've shined through your internship, and you know to finish strong. Now keep shining into your career. I did quite a few internships as an undergraduate and of course wasn't hired at each place. But I'm still in touch with each and every company, as well as past intern supervisors/ bosses who have gone on to other companies, expanding all of our networks further.

Don't drop the ball at the end. Be respectful and diligent from your application process all the way through your internship, and you will have maximized every possible angle of your experience and beyond. I can't wait to see where all of this information takes you, your career, and where you go next.

KEY TAKEAWAYS

Give it your all until the last day of your internship. Just because your semester or entire college experience is coming to an end, you can't stop tuning in at your internship. Show up every day you typically work, and be as enthusiastic and helpful as possible. Finishing strong will solidify the great reputation you've been building all along.

Volunteer to help with the transition. As you prepare to wrap-up your internship, be proactive in assisting the new future interns in any way you can. Offer to make a list of your duties for the new interns, and let your supervisor know that you're available for the first month or so should anyone have questions or need anything. Your willingness to lend a hand will be remembered and appreciated.

Stay in touch to maintain your contacts—respectfully. Keep active on social media platforms and continue to foster relationships with the colleagues you bonded with during your internship. Also, request to meet with your supervisor to discuss your career prospects when you begin your job search. Continue going to public work events to network and foster new connections.

Send a sincere "thank you" note. A physical "thank you" note is a very thoughtful way to express gratitude in a modern era of emails. It will remind your supervisors what a hardworking, warm, and diligent person you are. This might also increase your odds of communicating with professionals in your field at just the right time when you are on the hunt for open positions in your field. Send a physical thank you note to show your gratitude. But also know that it is a great calling card to uniquely stand out and stay in touch for your benefit.

Conclusion

You are now ready to thrive at your internship! You are lucky to have this guide as a handbook and to know that Google searching is your friend anytime you need answers at your internships.

This book has provided you with the necessary skills and tips that will benefit you both at your internship(s) and in your career. These tips took me from a small town to where I wanted to go. And I am still going! Now you can, too.

As interning stories fill the headlines with drama and controversy, don't get discouraged and count yourself out before you've even started applying. Internships are currently the main way to get your foot in the door throughout various fields. By reading this book, you have a resource to navigate securing, financing, preparing for, and succeeding at your internships and careers.

You now have access to the modern tools and tips many assume you already know—even if they weren't taught in a traditional school setting. You know not to fear the phone. You're ready to "make yourself indispensable" at your internships and understand that you should ask before taking it upon yourself to be "proactive." You're ready to network and start building *your* brand—crucial and important skills at all levels of business. Above all, you know how to take care of yourself, both in and out of the workplace. This will help you finish strong at the end of your internship and for the rest of your life. You also have this book to reference whenever you're in doubt throughout your internship experiences.

Now, we want to hear from you. Head over to Interning 101's Facebook page (https://www.Facebook.com/Interning101), Twitter (https://Twitter.com/Interning101), and website (http://www.Interning101.com/) to share your internship experiences. Tag us (https://www.Instagram.com/Interning101/) in your Instagram photos from in and around your internships (with your supervisor's permission, of course). Let's all learn from each other to continue to grow throughout our careers. We can't wait to hear from you and celebrate your successes. Good luck! We're here to support you every step of the way via the above website and social platforms.

See you in the "real world"!

Made in the USA
Lexington, KY
09 September 2018